The Scientific
Nomenclature
of Birds in the
Upper Midwest

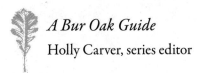

A Bur Oak Guide
Holly Carver, series editor

THE
SCIENTIFIC
NOMENCLATURE
OF

Birds

IN THE UPPER MIDWEST

James Sandrock and Jean C. Prior

UNIVERSITY OF IOWA PRESS, IOWA CITY

University of Iowa Press, Iowa City 52242

Copyright © 2014 by the University of Iowa Press

www.uiowapress.org

Printed in the United States of America

Design by April Leidig

The University of Iowa Press is a member of Green Press
Initiative and is committed to preserving natural resources.

Printed on acid-free paper

Library of Congress Cataloging-in-Publication Data

Sandrock, James P., 1929–

The scientific nomenclature of birds in the Upper Midwest /
by James Sandrock and Jean C. Prior.

pages   cm.— (A bur oak guide)

Includes bibliographical references and index.

ISBN 978-1-60938-225-4, 1-60938-225-0 (pbk.)

1. Birds — Middle West — Nomenclature. 2. Birds —
Middle West — Nomenclature (Popular).

I. Prior, Jean Cutler. II. Title.

QL683.M55S36   2014

598.0977 — dc23   2013021787

Contents

Acknowledgments

THIS CONTRIBUTION to the study of birds and their names follows a remarkable tradition begun gray years ago and carried on by many people who march through these pages: Aristotle, Pliny the Elder, Alexander Wilson, John James Audubon, and all the others who found birds, studied birds, named birds, and wrote about and painted birds. Their work, so fundamental to the discipline of ornithology, makes books like this possible.

The study of words for birds—their scientific and vernacular nomenclature—has its own linguistic and literary tradition. In addition to the writers of antiquity, we looked to Carolus Linnaeus, Elliott Coues, Mary Ferguson Coble, Ernest A. Choate, and many others who labored in the fields of philology, etymology, taxonomy, and terminology and cleared new paths through the babel of bird names. Especially helpful in the writing of this book were the works of Oscar E. Nybakken, James A. Jobling, W. Geoffrey Arnott, and Roland W. Brown.

Writers of field guides and references who have advanced the study and appreciation of birds by both illustrations and words provided valued and inspirational sources. We used and benefited from many but found ourselves most frequently reaching for the field guides of Richard Pough, David Sibley, and Donald and Lillian Stokes. Our daily reference companions were *The Encyclopedia of North American Birds*, by John K. Terres, and *Birds of America*, edited by T. Gilbert Pearson, John Burroughs, et al. Much of the biographical information in this book was based on the biographies in *Audubon to Xantus: The Lives of Those Commemorated in North American Bird Names*, by Barbara and Richard Mearns.

We also acknowledge those who have graciously given their time and expertise during the writing of this book. Richard M. Runge readily answered questions and offered suggestions about Germanic words, forms, and usages; Donald F. Jackson provided welcome counsel and guidance concerning Greek and Latin texts, etymologies, variant readings, and transliterations; Johanna K. Sandrock researched a legion of words and forms in Latin, Greek, and German, often by long distance. They have our respect and gratitude. Any errors in word or spirit that here occur are, of course, our own.

We wish to thank Charlotte Wright, managing editor of the University of Iowa Press, who shepherded this book through the labyrinthine publication process. We also express sincere gratitude to Cynthia Lindlof, who improved our manuscript with her knowledge, editorial skills, and appreciation of our purpose. And we especially thank Holly Carver, who encouraged this enterprise, then advised and cheered us along during the creation of the book now in your hand.

habent sua fata libelli:
"little books have their own destiny"

The Scientific
Nomenclature
of Birds in the
Upper Midwest

Introduction

THE NAMING OF THINGS may be the world's oldest profession. Adam was assigned the task in the second chapter of Genesis, and the nomenclature and taxonomy of biological organisms were the main occupations of early scientists. As a result, flocks of books treat these matters—from the works of Aristotle and Pliny the Elder to those of James A. Jobling and Joel Ellis Holloway. This book continues the long tradition of listing and explaining scientific, or "Latin," names.

A deep and long-standing interest in both birds and words has led us to the conviction that to know the meaning of the scientific names of birds, as well as their common and regional names, can be helpful in the identification and retention of the birds' distinguishing marks and traits. A Latin or Greek word can be as incandescent as the bird it describes; a folk name, as unique. We encourage birders of all skill levels to take this new reference in backpack or pocket to use with their favorite field guide, so to experience birds in prose as well as in pictures. Its use will not only enhance a day of birding but result in an accumulated knowledge and appreciation of birds.

The purpose of this book, then, is to list and explain the scientific names of birds that occur in one or more states of the Upper Midwest: Illinois, Indiana, Iowa, Kansas, Michigan, Minnesota, Missouri, Nebraska, North Dakota, Ohio, South Dakota, and Wisconsin. It should be pointed out, however, that many of these birds occur throughout the United States and that this handbook can be used by birders in other parts of the country. While we strive to provide accurate etymologies and cogent translations in efficient, compact entries, there are times when we linger over an especially interesting, clouded, or challenging name, resulting in a new or different explanation for the scientific nomenclature. Listed also are the common names and selected regional or folk names for the species. Scientific and common names in this book are from the *Checklist of North American Birds* (American Ornithologists' Union [AOU], 1998) with supplements, including the 53rd Supplement of July 2012.

We have attempted to write the entries so that they will be distinctive and interesting to read. Although this book is essentially a reference work with no continuing narrative, we hope that it will be worthy of casual reading beyond merely an entry or two.

What's in a Name?

The complete scientific name of a bird has four parts, including the author and the year of the legitimately published name. The full scientific name of the Barn Swallow, for example, is *Hirundo rustica* Linnaeus 1758. The first two parts, the binomial, are the main concern of this book.

The binomial is in Latin or postclassical Latin or is a latinized form printed in italics. The first element, *Hirundo*, is the genus (a group of related species), which is a form of a noun and capitalized. The second element, *rustica*, denotes the species (related birds within a genus), which is a form of an adjective in lowercase. The binomial (the scientific or "Latin" name) is assigned to this bird only and can be used for no other organism extant or extinct. This system has successfully adapted to the explosion of knowledge since its inception more than 200 years ago. Its stability—and resiliency—is unique.

In parsing a scientific name, we have given the Greek or Latin or latinized words that make up the binomial and have translated each component, when appropriate. For nouns and adjectives, we have determined the stem from the nominative singular, but when the stem is derived from the genitive singular, we have given that form in the text. The root of a verb is taken from the infinitive, and that form is given in the text. Greek words are transliterated according to the Romanization Table established by the Library of Congress and the American Library Association. We have neither accounted for the vowels that connect the two or more units of a compound word nor noted elision or linguistic incorrectness. We have not differentiated gender endings, even though gender is an important factor in scientific nomenclature. The Latin word for "yellow," for example, may appear as *flavus* (masculine), *flava* (feminine), or *flavum* (neuter). Any of these forms is translated "yellow" in the text. We have not included rules for the pronunciation of the scientific names. In general, they can be pronounced the same as in English, keeping in mind that each syllable is pronounced separately.

Carolus Linnaeus and other early authors called on a vast knowledge of both Greek and Latin, classical texts and literature— many obscure—when assigning names. Words and names from other languages, for example, Nahuatl, Quechuan, and Tupi, also have made their way into the taxonomic lexicon, thanks to early explorers of the Americas: words such as *pipixcan*, *chihi*, *anhinga*, and *piranga*. Latinized eponyms appear frequently in scientific names: *swainsonii*, *henslowii*. Place-names are abundant: *carolinensis*, *americana*. These names frequently indicate the location of the type specimen, that is, the individual bird on which the original scientific description and taxonomy were based. That there are occasionally words that are misspelled, whimsical, or even nonsensical; mistakes in grammar; and misnomers can add to the problems—and the charm—of interpreting these names.

The importance of the Linnaean system is that it establishes an internationally recognized label that distinguishes each discrete species from every other plant or animal in the world. The scientific name transcends all linguistic and political boundaries. An American might refer to a Barn Swallow, but the bird is known as *Rauchschwalbe* in Germany, *Hirondelle rustique* in France, *Golondrina tijereta* in Mexico, *Ladusvala* in Sweden, and *Tsunambe* in Japan. To the scientists in any country, in any language, the binomial *Hirundo rustica* is the recognized name.

We have placed the birds in a family, a designation that appears after every genus entry. These family names do not follow the formal scientific classification but rather reflect our experience in the field. At the first glimpse or call of a bird, we might say the family name, "sparrow" or "hawk" or "warbler," before sorting through our mental list of distinguishing marks to arrive at an identification of the species. We have generally followed the family names established by Richard H. Pough in his excellent field guides. We think they will help the reader to classify and identify birds in the field.

For each species, we have given the common name as it appears in the AOU Checklist. There follow under the rubric "Other names" a few regional or folk names for the species that can provide additional helpful tips to bird identification. The name "black-capped warbler," for example, is much more descriptive and memorable than either the scientific name *Cardellina wilsonia* or the common name Wilson's Warbler.

In choosing the birds to include in this book, we have consulted the AOU Checklist and supplements, checklists of the American Birding Association (ABA), regional and state checklists, field guides, range maps, and distribution studies. These sources vary considerably in criteria, content, and scale. Because of these variations, we did not attempt to provide an all-inclusive listing of birds in the Upper Midwest. We have included those species that we consider to occur regularly, casually—or sometimes accidentally—in one or more of the 12 states of the region.

The Law of Priority

The Law of Priority is a basic rule essential to the regulation of scientific nomenclature. This law states that the earliest scientific name properly assigned to an organism is distinct from all others and stands inviolate so long as it is scientifically valid, even if later found to be inaccurate. Mistakes in spelling, grammar, geography, characteristics, myths, and etymology are retained. Such errors do not affect the function of a scientific name or label. The Law of Priority dates from January 1, 1758, the date of Linnaeus's *Systema Naturae*, 10th edition.

If scientifically or taxonomically necessary, a bird can be moved to a new or different genus. Such action is becoming more and more the case with the discoveries now being made by DNA analyses. Even when the genus is changed, however, the name of a species remains unchanged. An example of such nomenclatural treatment is that of the Chestnut-sided Warbler. Originally named *Motacilla pensylvanica* in 1766, this species was subsequently placed in another genus and named *Dendroica pensylvanica*. Still another shift to another genus occurred in 2011, when the warbler was named *Setophaga pensylvanica*. Even though scientific analyses brought about the taxonomic shifts over the years, thus changing the genus, the specific name *pensylvanica* was retained—misspelling and all—by the Law of Priority.

Similar action takes place when a species later becomes a genus. The Northern Cardinal, for example, was originally named *Loxia cardinalis* in 1758. The species was subsequently determined to be a separate genus, *Cardinalis*, replacing *Loxia*. The species name *cardinalis* was retained by the Law of Priority, resulting in the current name, *Cardinalis cardinalis*. This binomial is called a tautonym, that is, "same name." Other tautonyms are *Xanthocephalus xanthocephalus*, *Riparia riparia*, *Perdix perdix*, and so on.

How to Use This Book

This book generally follows the format used by Mary Ferguson Coble and Cora Smith Life in their 91-page *Introduction to Ornithological Nomenclature* (Los Angeles, 1932) and in the 1954 edition by Coble. Her practical, alphabetical listing of bird names presented the etymological information ready to hand for the user, even—perhaps especially—in the field. Coble's small, flexibly bound vade mecum was easily carried in a pocket or backpack. Using Coble's basic pattern, we have given the etymologies of genus and species, the most frequently sought and most helpful names. In this book, the genera (capitalized) are listed alphabetically, as are the species (lowercase) below them. Both genus and species are italicized, for example:

CATHARUS
　fuscescens
　guttatus
　minimus
　ustulatus

The reader will easily locate the scientific name of the bird in question and its etymology, translation, and explanation by first going to the genus *CATHARUS* and then to the species below, *fuscescens* to *ustulatus*, all in alphabetical order. Both the species names and common names are listed alphabetically in separate indexes.

While Coble dedicated sections to eponyms, place-names, markings, habitat, and the like, we have included such information within the individual entries. The only dedicated section in this book is an appendix of short biographies of those people who were especially important in the nomenclature of birds. For reasons of space and readability, we have not included within the text footnote citations to our sources, all of which are listed in the bibliography.

It is our hope that readers will find this book rewarding when read at leisure and valuable when used in the field.

The Birds

ACANTHIS: A latinized form of Greek *akanthis*, Aristotle's word for "a kind of finch." FINCH FAMILY.

flammea: A Latin word for "flame-colored" that refers to the reddish tint on the forehead and breast, which may vary with age and season from pink to bright red.

COMMON NAME: Common Redpoll, a bird that can be seen regularly within its northern range

OTHER NAMES: little redpoll, mealy redpoll

hornemanni: The latinized form of "Hornemann's." This species was named for Jens Wilken Hornemann (1770–1841), a Danish botanist and author of *Flora Danica*, by his friend Carl Peter Holböll (1795–1856), a Danish explorer and administrator of Greenland, where the type specimen was collected.

COMMON NAME: Hoary Redpoll for the pale gray to white undertail coverts and rump; a "frosty" *A. flammea*

OTHER NAMES: arctic redpoll, Greenland redpoll, Hornemann's redpoll

ACCIPITER: This Latin word for "hawk" is derived from *accipere* = to take possession of, to grasp. The similar Greek word *okypteros* (from *ōkys* = swift + *pteron* = wing), i.e., "swift wing," is the general term for a bird of prey. Thus, "capturer" is an apt translation for this bird, which takes and kills prey with its talons. The more poetic translation "swift wing" would account for speed in the pursuit and quick disposal of prey. HAWK FAMILY.

cooperii: A latinized form of "Cooper's." This species was named for William Cooper (1798–1864), an American zoologist, bird collector, and a friend of Charles Lucien Jules Laurent Bonaparte (1803–1857), who described and named this species.

COMMON NAME: Cooper's Hawk

OTHER NAMES: striker, big blue darter, quail hawk

gentilis: Latin for "belonging to the same family or clan [*gens*]." By the mid-fourteenth century, the word had come to mean "of noble rank, superior, distinguished." Here, "noble" is an allusion to the size, appearance, flight, and courage of this audacious raptor, which was one of the birds so classified by medieval falconers.

COMMON NAME: Northern Goshawk for its general range in the United States and Canada; *gos* = goose, the reputed prey

OTHER NAMES: goose hawk, blue hen-hawk, blue darter, partridge hawk

striatus: Postclassical Latin for "streaked, lined" from *stria* = a furrow, line. "Streaked" refers to the vertical streaks of the underparts and the barred tail.

COMMON NAME: Sharp-shinned Hawk for the thin tarsus exposed below the short feathers on the upper leg

OTHER NAMES: little blue darter, bullet hawk, sharpie

ACTITIS: The Greek word *aktitēs* = dweller on the coast (*aktē*). "Shore habitué" describes the habitat. SANDPIPER FAMILY.

macularius: A postclassical Latin adjective from *macula* = spot, blot. "Marked with spots, speckled" refers to the small dark dotting on the white underparts.

COMMON NAME: Spotted Sandpiper

OTHER NAMES: teeter-tail, tip-up, sand lark

AECHMOPHORUS: From Greek *aichmophoros* = carrying a spear (*aichmē*). "Spear bearer" alludes to the long, sharp shape of the bill. GREBE FAMILY.

clarkii: A latinized word for "Clark's." John Henry Clark (ca. 1830–ca. 1885) was a member of the United States and Mexican Boundary Survey (1851–1855) and other expeditions during which he collected many specimens for the Smithsonian Institution.

COMMON NAME: Clark's Grebe

OTHER NAMES: None found

occidentalis: The Latin word for "westerly, western" denotes the general range of this bird in the United States and Canada.

COMMON NAME: Western Grebe

OTHER NAMES: swan-necked grebe, western dabchick

AEGOLIUS: Greek *aigōlios* = a small owl (Aristotle); Latin *aegolios* = a kind of screech owl (Pliny). In Greek myth, Aigolios was one of Zeus's nurses, who was transformed into a "bird of omen"—perhaps an owl? OWL FAMILY.

acadicus: A latinized form of "Acadian" designates the region of the type specimen taken in Acadia, i.e., Nova Scotia.

COMMON NAME: Northern Saw-whet Owl for the breeding range and for the call during breeding season, which, it is said, resembles the sound of a saw being sharpened

OTHER NAMES: saw-filer, whetsaw, white-fronted owl

funereus: The Latin word for "of a funeral, funereal" captures the call, a regular, mournful sound like that of a death knell.

COMMON NAME: Boreal Owl for its range in northern forests

OTHER NAMES: arctic saw-whet owl, tooting owl, little owl

AERONAUTES: From Greek *aēr, aeros* (genitive) = air, atmosphere + *nautēs* = seaman, sailor. "Sailor of the air" alludes to this bird's exceptional flying skills. Birds of this genus, possibly the fastest of North American birds, fly higher and faster and glide longer than other swifts. SWIFT FAMILY.

saxatalis: The Latin adjective for "dwelling among rocks" describes a bird that occupies cliffs and steep canyons during the summer months.

COMMON NAME: White-throated Swift for the white throat and underparts

OTHER NAME: rock swift

AGELAIUS: From Greek *agelaios* = belonging to a herd, gregarious. "Social" aptly describes the behavior of assembling in large, shifting flocks. BLACKBIRD FAMILY.

phoeniceus: The Latin word for "purple-red" (Greek *phoinikeos*) highlights the bright red "epaulets" on the wings of the adult male.

COMMON NAME: Red-winged Blackbird

OTHER NAMES: marsh blackbird, red-shouldered blackbird

AIX: The Greek word for "goat," but this word is used by Aristotle for an unidentified waterbird: suggestions include plover, snipe, teal, grebe, and—owl! DUCK FAMILY.

sponsa: Latin word for "bride, betrothed" (from *spondēre* = to promise, pledge). This adjective, although feminine, applies to the lovely "bridal" plumage of the adult breeding male.

COMMON NAME: Wood Duck for the preferred habitat of this bird, which nests in tree cavities

OTHER NAMES: woody, squealer, the bride

AMMODRAMUS: From Greek *ammos* = sand, a sandy place + *dramein* = to run. "Sand runner" pertains to the shy behavior of birds in this genus, which run rather than fly when disturbed in their grassland habitat. SPARROW FAMILY.

bairdii: A latinized form of "Baird's." This bird was named for Spencer F. Baird.

COMMON NAME: Baird's Sparrow

OTHER NAMES: None found

henslowii: A latinized form of "Henslow's." John Stevens Henslow (1796–1861) was a British clergyman, naturalist, and professor at Cambridge University and taught Charles Darwin, whom he recommended for the position of naturalist on the HMS *Beagle.*

COMMON NAME: Henslow's Sparrow

OTHER NAME: Henslow's bunting

leconteii: This bird was named by John James Audubon for John Lawrence Le Conte (1825–1883), an American physician and entomologist.

COMMON NAME: Le Conte's Sparrow

OTHER NAME: Le Conte's bunting

nelsoni: A latinized form of "Nelson's." Edward William Nelson (1885–1934) was founding president of the AOU and chief of the US Biological Survey.

COMMON NAME: Nelson's Sparrow

OTHER NAMES: Nelson's sharp-tailed sparrow, Nelson's finch

savannarum: A latinized form (genitive plural) of Spanish *zavana* = an open, treeless plain, i.e., savanna. "Of the plains" perfectly describes this bird's grassland habitat.

COMMON NAME: Grasshopper Sparrow for its insectlike, high-pitched, buzzing song

OTHER NAMES: grass dodger, quail sparrow

ANAS: Latin for "a duck." DUCK FAMILY.

acuta: This Latin word for "sharp, pointed" describes the long, spiked tail.

COMMON NAME: Northern Pintail for the breeding range in the United States and Canada and for the prominent, tapering tail feathers

OTHER NAMES: sprig, spike-tail, sprit-tail

americana: A latinized form of "American," which distinguishes this bird from the Eurasian species (*A. penelope*).

COMMON NAME: American Wigeon

OTHER NAMES: baldpate, blue-billed wigeon, green-headed wigeon

clypeata: The Latin word for "armed with a shield [*clipeus*]" alludes to the shape of the bill.

COMMON NAME: Northern Shoveler for the general breeding range in the northern (and western) United States and Canada and for the shape and use of the bill

OTHER NAMES: spoonbill, scooper, mud duck

crecca: This specific term was applied very early to this bird by Linnaeus in his *Fauna Suecica* (1746). It is apparently a latinized form of the characteristic utterance of the male, perhaps *crek* or *crüc.* Similar onomatopoetic names for the Green-winged Teal are the Swedish *kricka*, Danish *krikand*, and German *Krickente*, all of which seem to confirm the etymology as echoic. It is difficult to exclude Greek *krex* and Latin *crex*; both are rail-like birds named for their raspy sounds.

COMMON NAME: Green-winged Teal for the prominent green speculum, especially visible in flight

OTHER NAMES: redhead teal, mud teal, winter teal

cyanoptera: From Greek *kyaneos* = (dark) blue + *pteron* = feather, wing. "Blue wing" refers to the prominent blue patches on the forewings.

COMMON NAME: Cinnamon Teal for the general color of the plumage

OTHER NAMES: red-breasted teal, red teal

discors: Latin for "discordant, inharmonious," which apparently alludes to the utterances made when taking flight. The calls of this bird, however, are not unpleasing.

COMMON NAME: Blue-winged Teal for the sky-blue wing patches on the forewings, most visible in flight

OTHER NAMES: white-faced teal, summer teal, fall duck

fulvigula: From Latin *fulvus* = dark, tawny + *gula* = throat. "Tawny throat" describes the light brown color of the neck.

COMMON NAME: Mottled Duck for the variegated plumage

OTHER NAMES: black mallard, dusky duck

penelope: From the Greek *pēnelops* = a kind of duck. According to Elliott Coues, Linnaeus used the Greek word for "duck" when naming this species and not the name of Odysseus's faithful wife, Penelope. In Greek myth, Penelope's parents cast her into the sea, where she was fed and saved by ducks (*pēnelopes*), hence her name.

COMMON NAME: Eurasian Wigeon, which distinguishes this species from its American counterpart (*A. americana*)

OTHER NAMES: European wigeon, whistler, whewer

platyrhynchos: From Greek *platys* = flat, wide + *rhynchos* = bill, beak, nose. "Broad-billed" describes the large beak.

COMMON NAME: Mallard, derived from Old French and Old English *malard* = drake; anglicized to "mallard"

OTHER NAMES: common wild duck, curly-tail, green-head

querquedula: Latin for "a kind of duck" is an onomatopoetic name. "Little quacker" applies to the call.

COMMON NAME: Garganey. Another onomatopoetic name from the root *garg*, which suggests the throat sounds of Greek *gargarizein* = to gargle; Middle French *gargouiller* = to gurgle; Italian *garganello* = throat. *Garganello* is also an Italian dialect name for this duck.

OTHER NAME: Garganey teal

rubripes: From Latin *ruber* = red + *pes* = foot. "Red-footed" refers to the reddish-orange feet and legs.

COMMON NAME: American Black Duck for its range and dark brown plumage

OTHER NAMES: dusky mallard, red-legged duck, blackjack

strepera: A coined adjective from Latin *strepere* = to make a noise, clatter, or clang. "Noisy" expresses the loud call.

COMMON NAME: Gadwall. The etymology is uncertain, but the word has been in use since the 1600s.

OTHER NAMES: gray duck, creek duck, bleating duck

ANHINGA: The Tupi (Brazil) name for this bird. This and many other Tupi words for natural phenomena are found in

Historia Naturalis Brasiliae (1648; see *Platalea ajaja*). ANHINGA FAMILY.

anhinga: A tautonym.

COMMON NAME: Anhinga

OTHER NAMES: water turkey, snake bird, darter

ANSER: The Latin word for "goose." GOOSE FAMILY.

albifrons: From Latin *albus* = white + *frons* = forehead, brow, front. "White front" refers to the white forehead of the adult.

COMMON NAME: Greater White-fronted Goose, which is larger than the Eurasian Lesser White-fronted Goose (*A. erythropus*)

OTHER NAMES: specklebelly, laughing goose, yellow-legged goose

ANTHUS: Latin for "a small grassland bird" (Pliny) and Greek *anthos* = a small, beautifully colored bird (Aristotle). In Greek myth, Anthos was killed by horses. Zeus, out of pity, changed him into a bird. SPARROW FAMILY.

rubescens: A form of Latin *rubescere* = to become red, i.e., slightly red. "Reddish" refers to the buffy breast, especially of the Upper Midwest group.

COMMON NAME: American Pipit to distinguish this species from its Eurasian counterparts

OTHER NAMES: water pipit, wagtail, brown lark

spragueii: A latinized form of "Sprague's." This bird was named for Isaac Sprague (1811–1895), an American botanical and ornithological illustrator who was a member of Audubon's last expedition in 1843 to the Upper Missouri.

COMMON NAME: Sprague's Pipit

OTHER NAME: prairie skylark

ANTROSTOMUS: From Greek *antron* = cave, cavern (Latin *antrum*) + *stoma* = mouth. "Cavernous mouth" alludes to the large, gaping mouth of birds in this genus. NIGHTJAR FAMILY.

carolinensis: A coined Latin adjective for "Carolina" + suffix *-ensis* = of or from a place. "Of the Carolinas" identifies the region where the type specimen was collected.

COMMON NAME: Chuck-will's-widow for an imitation of the call

OTHER NAMES: the great bat, chick-a-willa, mosquito hawk

vociferus: From Latin *vox, vocis* (genitive) = voice + *ferre* = to carry, bear. "Noisy, loud, clamorous" verifies the loud, persistent call.

COMMON NAME: Eastern Whip-poor-will for its range and an onomatopoetic rendering of its call

OTHER NAMES: cave-mouth, mimic

APHELOCOMA: From Greek *aphelēs* = smooth, level, plain + *komē* (Latin *coma*) = the hair of the head. "Smooth hair" refers to the lack of a crest. JAY FAMILY.

californica: A latinized adjective meaning "of or from California," which designates the locality of the type specimen taken at Monterey.

COMMON NAME: Western Scrub-Jay for the general range and habitat

OTHER NAMES: long-tailed jay, California jay

AQUILA: Latin word for "eagle." HAWK FAMILY.

chrysaetos: From Greek *chryseos* = golden, gold-colored + *aetos* = eagle. "Golden eagle" highlights the gold-tinged nape of the adult.

COMMON NAME: Golden Eagle

OTHER NAMES: mountain eagle, brown eagle, war eagle

ARCHILOCHUS: One of several hummingbird genera named by Heinrich Gottlieb Reichenbach (1793–1879), a German botanist and ornithologist, who wished to commemorate classical Greek figures. Archilochus was an innovative, radical Greek soldier-poet who lived ca. 700 B.C. HUMMINGBIRD FAMILY.

alexandri: Latin for "Alexandre's." This bird was named in 1846 for M. M. Alexandre, a French physician. According to one source, he collected the type specimen in the Sierra Madre of western Mexico. Little information exists about Alexandre and his collecting activities.

COMMON NAME: Black-chinned Hummingbird for the distinct dark band across the chin and above the iridescent violet lower throat of the adult male

OTHER NAMES: black-chin, black-chinned hummer

colubris: A latinized form of *colibri*, an Arawak/Taíno (Caribbean) word for "little magic one, spirit one," i.e., a hummingbird.

COMMON NAME: Ruby-throated Hummingbird for the iridescent ruby-red gorget

OTHER NAMES: hummer, ruby-throat

ARDEA: The Latin word for "heron." HERON FAMILY.

alba: Latin for "white," which describes the plumage color of this wading bird.

COMMON NAME: Great Egret for the largest egret in the United States

OTHER NAMES: American egret, plume bird, long white

herodias: From Greek *erōdios* = heron. Both the Latin genus and Greek species names mean "heron"—a classically named bird.

COMMON NAME: Great Blue Heron for this bluish heron, the largest in the United States and Canada

OTHER NAMES: blue crane, big cranky

ARENARIA: The Latin word for "sandy" refers to the shoreline habitat. SANDPIPER FAMILY.

interpres: Latin for "agent, messenger." The allusion, apparently, is to the alarm call, warning other birds of impending danger.

COMMON NAME: Ruddy Turnstone for the reddish-brown on the back and wings and for the habit of flipping small stones and other flotsam while searching for food

OTHER NAMES: calico jacket, checkered snipe, chuckatuck

ASIO: Latin for "a kind of horned owl," according to Pliny. Coues suggests that *asio* may be a Hebrew word of unknown meaning. OWL FAMILY.

flammeus: The Latin word for "flame-colored" is an exaggerated description of the mostly tawny plumage.

COMMON NAME: Short-eared Owl for the small, seldom seen, closely set "ear" tufts of feathers

OTHER NAMES: marsh owl, bog owl, prairie owl

otus: Pliny's word (Greek *ōtos*) for "a horned or eared owl." In this case, "eared" refers to the elongated feather tufts.

COMMON NAME: Long-eared Owl

OTHER NAMES: cat owl, cedar owl, little horned owl

ATHENE: Greek *Athēna*, the goddess of wisdom, war, and the arts, was frequently depicted with the Little Owl (*glaux*), another bird (*A. noctua*) in this genus. OWL FAMILY.

cunicularia: A Latin feminine form meaning "miner, burrower." The Latin word is from *cuniculus* = rabbit or burrow. The allusion is to the underground nesting sites.

COMMON NAME: Burrowing Owl

OTHER NAMES: ground owl, prairie-dog owl, long-legged owl

AYTHYA: From Greek *aithyia* = a seabird, diver. DUCK FAMILY.

affinis: The Latin word for "related to, connected with" refers to this duck's affinity with the Greater Scaup (*A. marila*).

COMMON NAME: Lesser Scaup. This species is only slightly smaller than the Greater Scaup. A Scottish dialect form of "scalp," scaup are beds of sand and small rocks on which shellfish breed. This bird feeds on mollusks, crustaceans, and aquatic vegetation found in such places.

OTHER NAMES: bluebill, raft duck, blackhead

americana: This latinized adjective form for "American" refers to the bird's general range in North and Central America.

COMMON NAME: Redhead for the rich red head of the male in breeding plumage

OTHER NAMES: reddy, grayback, raft duck

collaris: Latin for "pertaining to the neck." The translation "collared" alludes to the subtle brownish "ring" that demarcates the neck and breast but is difficult to see in the field; the white ring of the bill is a more obvious field mark.

COMMON NAME: Ring-necked Duck

OTHER NAMES: ringbill, moonbill, marsh bluebill

fuligula: From Latin *fuligo* = soot + *gula* = throat. "Sooty neck" pertains to the black neck and breast of the adult male.

COMMON NAME: Tufted Duck for the streaming feathers at the back of the crown of the adult male and a shorter tuft on the female

OTHER NAME: pochard

marila: A latinized form of Greek *marilē* = embers of charcoal. Here the dark gray of charcoal describes the predominant color on the back of breeding males.

COMMON NAME: Greater Scaup, which is somewhat larger than the Lesser Scaup (*A. affinis*)

OTHER NAMES: big bluebill, big blackhead, flock duck

valisineria: Alexander Wilson named this species for its preferred diet of wild celery (*Vallisneria americana*), a type of grass. Linnaeus named this genus of grasses for Antonio Vallisneri (1661–1730), an Italian physician and naturalist. The misspelling is retained by the Law of Priority.

COMMON NAME: Canvasback for plumage, which resembles the color and appearance of canvas fabric

OTHER NAMES: can, canny, gray duck

BAEOLOPHUS: From Greek *baios* = little, slight, small + *lophos* = tuft or crest on the head of a bird. "Small tuft" refers to the relatively short crest. CHICKADEE FAMILY.

bicolor: The Latin word for "two-colored" is a description of the predominantly gray and white plumage.

COMMON NAME: Tufted Titmouse for the small crest

OTHER NAMES: crested titmouse, tomtit, peter bird (for call)

BARTRAMIA: A latinized form of "Bartram's." This genus was named for William Bartram (1739–1823), an American botanist, naturalist, and artist. A skilled ornithologist, Bartram traveled widely in the southeastern United States. In 1791, he published his classic work *Travels through North and South Carolina, Georgia, East and West Florida, the Cherokee Country, the Extensive Territories of the Muscogulges or Creek Confederacy, and the Country of the Chactaws, Containing an Account of the Soil and Natural Productions of Those Regions, Together with Observations on the Manners of the Indians*, in which he reported having seen 215 bird species. Bartram greatly influenced the young Alexander Wilson. SANDPIPER FAMILY.

longicauda: From Latin *longus* = long + *cauda* = tail. "Long-tailed" calls attention to the tail, which extends beyond the wing tips at rest and is especially noticeable in flight.

COMMON NAME: Upland Sandpiper for the inland breeding range

OTHER NAMES: upland plover, pasture plover, prairie snipe

BOMBYCILLA: From Greek and Latin *bombyx* = silkworm, made of silk + spurious Latin *cilla* = tail. "Silky tail" apparently alludes to the glowing dash of yellow on the tip of the tail. WAXWING FAMILY.

cedrorum: From Latin *cedrus* (Greek *kedros*) = cedar tree. "Of the cedars" refers to the evergreens that provide the favored berries.

COMMON NAME: Cedar Waxwing

OTHER NAMES: cedar bird, cherry bird

garrulus: Latin for "chattering, talkative." This is the generic name of the clamorous Eurasian Jay (*Garrulus glandarius*), which this bird is thought to resemble.

COMMON NAME: Bohemian Waxwing. Although the range of this bird does include Bohemia, this has no bearing on its name. "Bohemian" can refer to a wanderer or vagabond, both of which would describe the irruptive behavior of this species that appears and disappears seemingly at random within its range.

OTHER NAMES: black-throated waxwing, silktail, northern chatterer

BONASA: This is the feminine form of the Latin masculine *bonasus* and Greek *bonasos*, both of which mean "bull, aurochs." A common belief is that the sound of the loud drumming by the adult male grouse is similar to that of a bellowing bovine —female or male. GROUSE FAMILY.

umbellus: The masculine form of the Latin *umbella*, meaning "sunshade, parasol," is an allusion to the dark, expanded ruff of the breeding male. Coues suggests that *umbellata*, meaning "shaded," would be better Latin. That's true, but whatever irregularities occur in this and other such cases are retained by the Law of Priority.

COMMON NAME: Ruffed Grouse for the distinctive ruff displayed by the breeding male

OTHER NAMES: drummer, red grouse, pine hen, partridge

BOTAURUS: From Greek *boan* = to thunder, roar + *tauros* = bull. "Bull bellow" refers to the deep, resonant booming *gunk-gunk* call during breeding season. HERON FAMILY.

lentiginosus: From Latin *lentigo, lentiginis* (genitive) = lentil-shaped spot, freckle + suffix *-osus* = full of. "Full of freckles" describes the strongly streaked and spotted plumage, especially of the throat and breast.

COMMON NAME: American Bittern to distinguish this species from the Eurasian Bittern (*B. stellaris*)

OTHER NAMES: thunder pumper, bog bull, look-up

BRANTA: Most likely a latinized term from an Indo-European root meaning "to burn, to be consumed by fire," e.g., Old English *brænan*, Old Norse *brenna*. The suggestion that *Branta* is a corrupted latinized form of Greek *brenthos*, meaning "an unknown waterbird," seems a less likely possibility. "Burnt" refers to the dark, generally black and brown colors of plumage, which give the birds of this genus a "charred" appearance. GOOSE FAMILY.

bernicla: The postclassical Latin word for "barnacle," from which, according to legend, these birds were thought to hatch. The shape and color of these crustaceans, together with their streaming, feathery cirri, which resemble a bird's plumage, seemed gooselike to the ancients.

COMMON NAME: Brant

OTHER NAMES: burnt goose, clatter goose, quink, wavey

canadensis: Coined Latin adjective for "Canada" + suffix *-ensis* = of or from a place. "From Canada" identifies the breeding range and the locality of the type specimen collected near the city of Quebec.

COMMON NAME: Canada Goose

OTHER NAMES: calling goose, honker, wild goose

hutchinsii: A latinized form of "Hutchins's." This species was named for Thomas Hutchins (died 1790), a Hudson Bay Company surgeon who collected birds in the Hudson Bay area.

COMMON NAME: Cackling Goose for the high-pitched, clamorous call of some of the many groups in this complex

OTHER NAMES: little goose, little Canada goose

BUBO: Latin word for "horned owl" (Greek *bouphos* = a species of owl). Both the Latin and Greek words contain the onomatopoetic *oo* sound of an owl call. "Hooter" expresses the low-pitched calls. OWL FAMILY.

scandiacus: Coined Latin adjective for "Scandia" = Scandinavia + suffix *-acus* = of or pertaining to. "Of Scandinavia" identifies the locality of the type specimen taken in Lapland.

COMMON NAME: Snowy Owl for the mostly white plumage of the adult male and for the very northern range in both North America and Eurasia

OTHER NAMES: great white owl, ermine owl, arctic owl

virginianus: Coined Latin adjective for "Virginia" + suffix *-anus* = of or from. "Of Virginia" identifies the colonial region where the type specimen was collected in 1788.

COMMON NAME: Great Horned Owl for the large size and prominent tufts of feathers ("horns") on the crown

OTHER NAMES: big hoot owl, tiger owl, eagle owl, king owl

BUBULCUS: Latin for "one who plows with an ox [*bos*]." The translation "herdsman" alludes to the behavior of this bird that follows cattle, feeding on insects kicked up by the grazing animals. HERON FAMILY.

ibis: A Greek and Latin word for "ibis." This species was apparently thought to resemble the ibis.

COMMON NAME: Cattle Egret

OTHER NAMES: buff-backed heron, cattle heron

BUCEPHALA: From Greek *bous* = bull, ox, cow + *kephalē* = the head. "Bull-headed" points out the relatively large head-to-body ratio, similar in proportion to that of the American bison. DUCK FAMILY.

albeola: From Latin *albus* = white + diminutive suffix *-ola*. "Little white" refers to the white patch on the head.

COMMON NAME: Bufflehead for the oversized head, like that of a buffalo

OTHER NAMES: butterball, black and white duck, bumblebee duck

clangula: From Latin *clangor* (Greek *klangē*) = noise, sound, clang + diminutive suffix *-ula*. "Little noise" is thought to describe the distinct sound of the wings in flight.

COMMON NAME: Common Goldeneye for the bright yellow iris of a bird that is common throughout the United States and Canada

OTHER NAMES: whistle wing, jingler, merry wing

islandica: A latinized form of "Islandia" = Iceland + suffix *-ica* = of or pertaining to. "Of Iceland" identifies the location of the type specimen.

COMMON NAME: Barrow's Goldeneye for the eye color and for John Barrow (1764–1848), a secretary of the British Admiralty and a founder of the Royal Geographic Society, who supported many Arctic expeditions, most notably the search for the Northwest Passage

OTHER NAMES: Rocky Mountain goldeneye, whistle-diver

BUTEO: The Latin word for "a kind of hawk, falcon, or buzzard." HAWK FAMILY.

jamaicensis: Coined Latin adjective for "Jamaica" + suffix *-ensis* = of or from a place. "Of Jamaica" indicates where the type specimen was collected.

COMMON NAME: Red-tailed Hawk for the red to reddish-brown color of the tail in almost all morphs

OTHER NAMES: redtail, hen hawk, buzzard hawk

lagopus: From Greek *lagos* = hare + *pous* = foot. "Hare-foot" refers to the feather-covered legs, which resemble the fur on the legs and feet of, for example, a snowshoe hare.

COMMON NAME: Rough-legged Hawk for the shaggy appearance of the feathered legs

OTHER NAMES: rough-leg, mouse hawk

lineatus: Latin word for "striped, decked out." "Striped" describes the narrow white bands on the tail and the red, white, and brown streaking on the underparts. "Decked out" is also apt for the appearance of this striking bird.

COMMON NAME: Red-shouldered Hawk for the reddish to buff patch on the shoulder

OTHER NAMES: brown hawk, red-bellied hawk, winter hawk

platypterus: From Greek *platys* = flat, wide + *pteron* = wing. "Broad wing" characterizes the perceived width of the wing.

COMMON NAME: Broad-winged Hawk

OTHER NAME: broad-winged buzzard

regalis: The Latin word for "royal, regal" describes well this large, powerful species of *Buteo* and the locality of its type specimen collected at Real del Monte, Hidalgo, Mexico.

COMMON NAME: Ferruginous Hawk for the plumage, which is the color of rust (Latin *ferrugo*)

OTHER NAMES: prairie hawk, squirrel hawk, gopher hawk

swainsoni: Latin for "Swainson's." This bird was named for British ornithologist William Swainson.

COMMON NAME: Swainson's Hawk

OTHER NAMES: brown-throated hawk, black hawk, grasshopper hawk

BUTORIDES: From Latin *butio* and Old French *butor* = bittern + Greek suffix *-oides* = similar to, resembling. "Bittern-like" pertains to the mottled feathering and heavily streaked brown throat of the juvenal plumage. HERON FAMILY.

virescens: A form of Latin *virescere* = to become green, i.e., slightly green. "Greenish" describes the bluish-green back of the adult.

COMMON NAME: Green Heron

OTHER NAMES: green-backed heron, fly-up-the-creek, shitepoke

CALAMOSPIZA: From Greek *kalamos* = reed + *spiza* = finch. "Reed finch" is intended to describe the habitat of this grassland genus. SPARROW FAMILY.

melanocorys: From Greek *melas*, *melanos* (genitive) = black + a form of Greek *korys* = a kind of lark. "Black lark" refers to the predominant color of the adult male and the larklike song.

COMMON NAME: Lark Bunting for the rich, varied song while hovering

OTHER NAMES: white-winged blackbird, buffalo bird

CALCARIUS: From Latin *calcar* = spur + suffix *-ius* = pertaining to or having. "Spurred" indicates the long nail on the hind toe. SPARROW FAMILY.

lapponicus: Coined adjective from postclassical Latin *Lapponia* = Lapland + suffix *-icus* = of or pertaining to. "Of Lapland" refers to the location where the type specimen was collected.

COMMON NAME: Lapland Longspur

OTHER NAMES: Alaska longspur, stubble sparrow, common longspur *ornatus:* Latin word for "well dressed, decked out," which describes the impressive breeding plumage of the adult male.

COMMON NAME: Chestnut-collared Longspur for the prominent reddish-brown band on the nape of the adult male

OTHER NAME: butterfly bird

pictus: Latin word for "painted, decorated, ornate," which alludes to the distinctive pattern and colors of the adult male's plumage.

COMMON NAME: Smith's Longspur. On his expedition to the Upper Missouri in 1843, Audubon collected this species and named it for his friend and sometime agent Gideon B. Smith (1793–1867), a silk entrepreneur from Baltimore. The type specimen, however, had been taken in Canada by Sir John Richardson on John Franklin's expedition of 1827 (see *Leucophaeus pipixcan*).

OTHER NAME: painted longspur

CALIDRIS: From Greek *(s)kalidris* = a gray, speckled waterbird (Aristotle). SANDPIPER FAMILY.

alba: The Latin word for "white" is the color of the winter plumage.

COMMON NAME: Sanderling, a name coined from "sand" and the German diminutive suffix *-ling,* i.e., "a little bird of the sand," which alludes to the beaches on which it is frequently seen

OTHER NAMES: beach bird, surf snipe, whitey, alouette

alpina: The Latin word for "alpine" refers to the breeding habitat in the alpine tundra life zone. The type specimen was collected in Lapland.

COMMON NAME: Dunlin from Old English *dunn* (Celtic and Gaelic *donn*) and words from other Indo-European languages meaning "dark" that describe the russet color on the back and scapulars, and the diminutive suffix -*lin*, thus "a little dark one"

OTHER NAMES: red-back, little black breast, crooked bill

bairdii: A latinized form of "Baird's" for Spencer F. Baird.

COMMON NAME: Baird's Sandpiper

OTHER NAMES: grass-bird, sand snipe

canutus: The Latin word for "frosty, gray and white" is an apt description of the juvenal plumage and of the adult plumage in winter. The conventional explanation for the species name *canutus* is that Linnaeus named this bird for King Canute of Denmark, who, according to legend, commanded the tide to stop. The tide, tidelike, continued to roll in and dampened the king's royal robes and feet. The foraging of this bird along the tide line reflects this legend. Both the Latin "frosty" and "Canute's bird" seem to have merit. The linguistic term, however, is likely of more help in identification than the legendary.

COMMON NAME: Red Knot for the color of breeding plumage and *knot*, an early form of Canute, which gives credence to the legend

OTHER NAMES: beach robin, redbreast, freckled sandpiper, silver-back

fuscicollis: From Latin *fuscus* = dark, dusky + *collis*, a postclassical Latin form of *collum* = neck. "Dark-necked" is a misnomer, since the neck of this species is not noticeably dark.

COMMON NAME: White-rumped Sandpiper for the distinctive white patch, most noticeable in flight

OTHER NAMES: beachy bird, sand-bird, mud snipe

himantopus: From Greek *himas, himantos* (genitive) = thong, strap + *pous* = foot. Pliny, among others, uses this word for a bird having long slender legs, implying that the legs are as long, thin, and leathery as a thong.

COMMON NAME: Stilt Sandpiper for the stiltlike legs

OTHER NAMES: long-legged sandpiper, frost snipe, bastard yellowlegs

maritima: A Latin word for "of the sea, seafaring, maritime," which describes the preferred coastal habitat.

COMMON NAME: Purple Sandpiper for the dark, purplish scapulars of the adult in winter plumage

OTHER NAMES: rock sandpiper, rockweed bird, rock snipe

mauri: A latinized form of "Mauri's." This species was named for Ernesto Mauri (1791–1836), an Italian botanist, by Jean Louis Cabanis (1816–1906), a German ornithologist who first described this bird in 1859.

COMMON NAME: Western Sandpiper for its range, mostly in the western half of the United States

OTHER NAME: snippet

melanotos: From Greek *melas* = black + *nōton* = the back. "Dark-backed" refers to the blackish streaks on the back, which are not much help when identifying this bird.

COMMON NAME: Pectoral Sandpiper for the bilateral air sacs on the breast and neck, which produce a low, booming mating call when inflated

OTHER NAMES: grass snipe, brown-back, squatter

minutilla: From Latin *minutus* = small + diminutive suffix *-illa* = small. "Very small" is an appropriate description of this, the smallest sandpiper.

COMMON NAME: Least Sandpiper, a reference to size, not importance

OTHER NAMES: mud-peep, sand-peep, ox-eye

pusilla: The Latin word for "very little" is an apt description of this species, one of the smaller sandpipers.

COMMON NAME: Semipalmated Sandpiper, referring to the partial (*semi*) webbing of the toes of the foot (here, *palma*)

OTHER NAMES: black-legged peep, little peep

CALLIPEPLA: From Greek *kalli* = beautiful + *peplos* and Latin *peplum* = robe, shawl, cloth. "Beautifully cloaked" characterizes the soft pearl-gray back, tail, and wings. QUAIL FAMILY.

squamata: This Latin word for "scaled" describes the intricate pattern of the feathers delicately edged in black on the underparts and neck, giving a squamous appearance.

COMMON NAME: Scaled Quail

OTHER NAMES: cotton top, blue quail, Mexican quail

CALYPTE: This is possibly a shortened form of Greek *kalyptrē* = a veil, covering. "Veiled" is perhaps an allusion to the adult male's rose-red crown and the gorget, which extends to the sides of the neck. HUMMINGBIRD FAMILY.

anna: This species was named by René Lesson (1794–1849), a French naturalist and ornithologist, for Anna Debelle Masséna (1802–1887), duchess of Rivoli and wife of Prince François Victor Masséna (1799–1863), an amateur ornithologist who had a private collection of more than 12,000 bird skins.

COMMON NAME: Anna's Hummingbird

OTHER NAME: Anna's hummer

CARDELLINA: From Latin *carduelis* = the thistle-bird, goldfinch + suffix *-ina*, which usually means "small, little" but may also indicate "likeness, belonging to." "Goldfinchlike" is probably not an exact term. Although the birds of this genus are small like goldfinches, they are long-winged, long-tailed ground nesters whose diet consists mainly of insects; it is difficult to make the connection with goldfinches. WARBLER FAMILY.

canadensis: Coined Latin adjective for "Canada" + suffix *-ensis* = of or from a place. "Of Canada" identifies the region where the type specimen was collected.

COMMON NAME: Canada Warbler

OTHER NAMES: necklaced warbler, speckled Canada warbler

pusilla: This Latin word for "very little" applies to one of the smallest warblers.

COMMON NAME: Wilson's Warbler, named for Alexander Wilson

OTHER NAMES: black-capped warbler, golden pileolated warbler, Wilson's flycatcher

CARDINALIS: From Latin *cardo, cardinis* (genitive) = hinge + suffix *-alis* = having the quality of. The name "cardinal" came to mean someone on whom things hinged or depended, i.e., someone or something important. In the Roman Catholic Church, the most important bishops wore scarlet robes and caps. This bird was named for its plumage, red as the garb of the ecclesiastical cardinals. CARDINAL FAMILY.

cardinalis: A tautonym.

COMMON NAME: Northern Cardinal for its range in the United States

OTHER NAMES: redbird, winter redbird, Virginia nightingale

CATHARTES: A latinized form of Greek *kathartēs* = purifier, purger. "Cleaner" refers to the scavenging behavior of these birds, which cleanse areas of carrion. VULTURE FAMILY.

aura: According to Coues, *aura* is a Mexican or South American Indian name for "vulture," which is somehow related to the Aztec word *urubu* or *ourubu*, meaning "(black) vulture." James A. Jobling posits the Mexican Indian word *auroura* as the name for this bird. Johannes de Laet (1581–1649), a Dutch geographer and cartographer, in his *Nieuwe Wereldt* (1625), writes that the *aura* is a high-flying, black bird that is able to smell fetid food from afar. It is possible that de Laet used the Latin word *aura* (a gentle breeze or shifting wind) as the name of this species, which soars high on rising thermals. Coble suggests that *aura* is a form of the Latin *aurum* (gold), perhaps an allusion to the "golden" climate and El Dorado legends of Vera Cruz, Mexico, where the type specimen was taken.

COMMON NAME: Turkey Vulture for the unfeathered head, dark plumage, and size, which resemble those of a turkey

OTHER NAMES: turkey buzzard, carrion crow

CATHARUS: From Greek *katharos* = pure, clean, spotless. The reason for this description is unclear; it may allude to the clear, flutey songs of birds in this genus or to their clean, immaculate white and brown plumage. THRUSH FAMILY.

fuscescens: A form of the inferred Latin verb *fuscescere* = to become dark (*fuscus*), i.e., slightly dark. "Darkish" indicates that this species is not so dark as others in this genus.

COMMON NAME: Veery, which is onomatopoetic

OTHER NAMES: ground thrush, tawny thrush, willow thrush

guttatus: From Latin *gutta* = a drop, natural spot, or speck + adjectival suffix *-atus* = provided with. "Spotted" refers to the dense, bold spots on the white or buffy breast.

COMMON NAME: Hermit Thrush for the reclusive behavior of this deep-woods bird

OTHER NAMES: rufous-tailed thrush, solitary thrush, evening bird, American nightingale

minimus: The Latin word for "smallest, least" is a misnomer, since this bird is slightly larger than other birds in this genus.

COMMON NAME: Gray-cheeked Thrush for the plain grayish to brownish "face"

OTHER NAME: Alice's thrush

ustulatus: A form of Latin *ustulāre* = to burn slightly, to singe. "Charred" describes the brownish-gray plumage, the color of ashes.

COMMON NAME: Swainson's Thrush, for William Swainson

OTHER NAMES: olive-backed thrush, russet-backed thrush, Alma's thrush

CATHERPES: From Greek *kata* = down + *herpein* = to creep. "Creeper" refers to the behavior of creeping down among the rocky ledges and crevices of canyon walls. WREN FAMILY.

mexicanus: Coined Latin adjective for "Mexico" + suffix -*anus* = of or from. "Of Mexico" identifies the locality of the type specimen collected at Hidalgo, Mexico.

COMMON NAME: Canyon Wren for the preferred habitat in deep, narrow gorges and canyons

OTHER NAMES: dotted wren, white-throated wren

CENTROCERCUS: From Greek *kentron* = point, spike + *kerkos* = tail. "Spike tail" is a description of the narrow, pointed tail feathers, which are especially visible when erected and fanned by the displaying male. GROUSE FAMILY.

urophasianus: From Greek *oura* = tail + *phasianos* = pheasant (see *Phasianus*). "Tail of a pheasant" refers to the long tail feathers, the longest of any North American grouse.

COMMON NAME: Greater Sage-Grouse (larger than *C. minimus*, Gunnison Sage-Grouse), named for its habitat, the sagebrush of arid plains where its diet is almost exclusively sage leaves in fall and winter

OTHER NAMES: sage hen, cock of the plains, sage chicken

CERTHIA: From Greek *kerthios* = a little bird living around trees (Aristotle). CREEPER FAMILY.

americana: A latinized form of "American" distinguishes this species from the Eurasian *C. familiaris.*

COMMON NAME: Brown Creeper for its color and behavior of creeping up tree trunks and limbs in search of food

OTHER NAMES: tree creeper, American creeper, common creeper

CHAETURA: Postclassical Latin *chaeta* = bristle, stiff hair (Greek *chaitē* = long, flowing hair) + Greek *oura* = tail. "Bristle tail" applies to the small, stiff hairs that extend beyond the tail feathers. SWIFT FAMILY.

pelagica: The Latin word (Greek *pelagios*), meaning "of the sea, marine," is a seemingly inappropriate appellation for this bird. This specific term has had a checkered etymological past. Linnaeus assigned the original binomial, *Hirundo pelagica*, in his authoritative *Systema Naturae* (10th ed., 1758). For some reason—whim? misspelling? misprint?—the name was changed in the 12th edition (1766) to *pelasgia*, possibly meaning "pertaining to the Pelasgi," an ancient, nomadic Aegean people, which could be an allusion to the wandering, migratory ways of this species. This name was used by Alexander Wilson, William Bartram, and others, but over the years various forms of the word made their way into print, e.g., *pelagtea*, *pelasgica*. The confusion was finally put to rest when the bird was moved from the genus *Hirundo* (swallow) to the genus *Chaetura* (swift) in 1825 and subsequently returned to the original *pelagica*. The allusion again is to the migration path of this species over the Caribbean Sea to its winter range in the headwaters of the Amazon River. The common name for this bird has an equally unstable history.

COMMON NAME: Chimney Swift for one of the common nesting sites

OTHER NAMES: chimney sweep, chimney swallow

CHARADRIUS: From Greek *charadrios* = a bird dwelling in ravines and gullies (*charadrai*), perhaps a stone-curlew. This bird appears in Aristotle and other sources. It may be a "thick-knee" or a kind of plover, but in translations of Deuteronomy 14:18, the bird is variously a cormorant, heron, or lapwing. In medieval bestiaries, it is depicted as an all-white bird, perhaps a plover. PLOVER FAMILY.

melodus: This Latin word (Greek *melōdos*) for "pleasantly singing" expresses the soft, clear, whistling calls.

COMMON NAME: Piping Plover for its musical calls

OTHER NAMES: sand plover, beach plover, pale ring-neck

montanus: The Latin word for "of a mountain," although the preferred habitat is on the high plains in open grasslands.

COMMON NAME: Mountain Plover

OTHER NAMES: prairie plover, field plover

nivosus: This Latin word for "full of snow, snowy" describes the very pale upperparts and white underparts.

COMMON NAME: Snowy Plover

OTHER NAMES: snowy ringed plover, western snowy plover

semipalmatus: From the Latin prefix *semi-* = half + *palmatus* = shaped like the palm of the hand (*palma*), a reference to the partially webbed toes

COMMON NAME: Semipalmated Plover

OTHER NAMES: ring-necked plover, beach bird, red-eye

vociferus: From Latin *vox, vocis* (genitive) = voice + *ferre* = to carry, to bear. "Noisy, loud, clamorous" expresses the loud, persistent call.

COMMON NAME: Killdeer, which is onomatopoetic

OTHER NAMES: chattering plover, noisy plover, killdee

wilsonia: A latinized form of "Wilson's." This bird is named for Alexander Wilson.

COMMON NAME: Wilson's Plover

OTHER NAME: thick-billed plover

CHEN: The Greek word for "goose." GOOSE FAMILY.

caerulescens: A form of the inferred Latin verb *caerulescere* = to become blue (*caeruleus*), i.e., slightly blue. This specific adjective is now applied to both the blue and the white morphs, once considered two species: *C. caerulescens,* the Blue Goose, named by Linnaeus in 1758; *C. hyperborea* (from Greek *hyper* = beyond + *boreas* = the north), the Snow Goose, named by Peter S. Pallas (1741–1811), a German naturalist and explorer. "Bluish" alludes to the appearance of the dark morph. This adjective, however, is not an accurate description of either morph, since some plumages in both are grayish-brown, especially on the adult dark morph.

COMMON NAME: Snow Goose for the adult plumage of the white morph

OTHER NAMES: white wavey, white goose, blue wavey, blue goose

rossii: The latinized form of "Ross's." This species was named for Bernard Rogan Ross (1827–1874), a chief factor of the Hudson Bay Company in Canada.

COMMON NAME: Ross's Goose

OTHER NAMES: horned wavey, little wavey

CHLIDONIAS: A mistransliteration of Greek *chelidōn* = a swallow + suffix *-ias* = having the quality of. The mistake is retained by the Law of Priority. "Swallowlike (bird)" describes the buoyant, dashing flight. Terns are commonly called "sea swallows." TERN FAMILY.

niger: The Latin word for "black" refers to the color of the head and body in breeding plumage.

COMMON NAME: Black Tern

OTHER NAMES: black sea swallow, sea pigeon, black gull

CHONDESTES: Greek *chondros* = grain, corn + *edestēs* = eater. "Grain eater" is a misnomer, since this monotype is insectivorous. SPARROW FAMILY.

grammacus: A latinized adjective form of *gramma* (Greek *grammē*) = a line (in writing). "Lined" refers to the facial markings.

COMMON NAME: Lark Sparrow for the rich, melodious song with a wide range, like that of a lark

OTHER NAMES: little meadowlark, lark finch, quail-head

CHORDEILES: From Greek *choros* = a choral, festive dance + *deilēs* = in the evening. "Twilight dance" captures the swirling sounds and flights of the birds in this genus as they search for insects at dusk. NIGHTJAR FAMILY.

minor: Latin for "smaller." This species is smaller than other nightjars known at the time it was described.

COMMON NAME: Common Nighthawk for this most regularly seen nighthawk in the United States

OTHER NAMES: bull-bat, swooper, moth hunter, pisk

CHROICOCEPHALUS: Greek *chroikos,* an unattested adjective form of *chroa* = color + *kephalē* = the head. "Colored head" refers to the dark brown to black head in breeding plumage. GULL FAMILY.

philadelphia: A latinized adjective meaning "from Philadelphia" identifies the locality of the type specimen collected near that city in Pennsylvania.

COMMON NAME: Bonaparte's Gull is named for the ornithologist Charles Lucien Jules Laurent Bonaparte (1803–1857), nephew of the French emperor. Charles Bonaparte spent eight years in America; his most significant scientific contributions concerned the taxonomy and nomenclature of birds.

OTHER NAMES: blackhead, mackerel gull

ridibundus: This Latin word for "laughing" conveys the call.

COMMON NAME: Black-headed Gull, which describes the color of the head in breeding plumage

OTHER NAMES: None found

CINCLUS: From Greek *kinklos* = a small waterbird (Aristotle and other writers of antiquity). DIPPER FAMILY.

mexicanus: Coined Latin adjective for "Mexico" + suffix *-anus* = of or from. "Of Mexico" identifies the locality where the type specimen was collected.

COMMON NAME: American Dipper, which distinguishes this bird from the Eurasian species (*C. cinclus*), both of which are at home in fast-flowing water

OTHER NAMES: water ouzel, slate bobber, water witch

CIRCUS: From Greek *kirkos* = a kind of hawk or falcon that flies in a circle (*kirkos*). HAWK FAMILY.

cyaneus: A latinized word from Greek *kyaneos* = (dark) blue for the pearl-gray plumage of the adult male, which appears to have a bluish cast.

COMMON NAME: Northern Harrier for the breeding range in the United States and Canada of this slim, narrow-winged hunter often seen gliding low over open fields

OTHER NAMES: marsh hawk, white-rumped hawk, blue harrier

CISTOTHORUS: From Greek *kistos* = shrub + *thouros* = leaping, rushing, impetuous. "Shrub leaper" aptly describes the habitat and bustling behavior of birds in this genus. WREN FAMILY.

palustris: Latin word for "of the swamp [*palus*]" refers to the low, marshy habitat of this bird.

COMMON NAME: Marsh Wren

OTHER NAMES: long-billed marsh wren, cattail wren, reed wren

platensis: Coined Latin combining *plata* = Río de la Plata + suffix *-ensis* = of or from a place. "From the Río de la Plata," near Buenos Aires, specifies where the type specimen was obtained.

COMMON NAME: Sedge Wren for the preferred habitat of sedges and grasses

OTHER NAMES: short-billed marsh wren, meadow wren, grass wren

CLANGULA: From Latin *clangor* (Greek *klangē*) = any sharp sound, the cry or scream of birds + diminutive suffix *-ula*. "Little chatterbox" expresses the perceived loquacity and yodeling of the male. DUCK FAMILY.

hyemalis: Latin for "of winter [*hiems*]" refers to the very northern breeding sites; these birds winter on both the Atlantic and Pacific coasts.

COMMON NAME: Long-tailed Duck for the streaming tail feathers of the adult male

OTHER NAMES: old-squaw, granny, scolder

COCCOTHRAUSTES: From Greek *kokkos* = kernel + *thrauein* = to shatter, break to pieces + suffix *-tēs* = agent, one that does. "Seed cracker" describes this bird and its method of harvesting seeds and buds from both coniferous and deciduous trees. GROSBEAK FAMILY.

vespertinus: The Latin word for "of or in the evening [*vesper*]" was applied to this bird, which was once believed to sing and be active in the evening.

COMMON NAME: Evening Grosbeak

OTHER NAMES: winter canary, sugar bird

COCCYZUS: From Greek *kokkyzein* = to call like a cuckoo (*kokkyx*). "Cuckoo" is onomatopoetic. CUCKOO FAMILY.

americanus: A coined latinized adjective form for "America" + suffix *-anus* = of or from. "Of America" locates its range in the Western Hemisphere.

COMMON NAME: Yellow-billed Cuckoo for the color of the bill below the culmen

OTHER NAMES: rain crow, storm crow, rain dove, kow-kow (for call)

erythropthalmus: From Greek *erythros* = red + *ophthalmos* = eye. The mistransliteration is retained by the Law of Priority. "Red-eyed" describes the orbital ring, not the eye.

COMMON NAME: Black-billed Cuckoo for the color of the bill

OTHER NAMES: rain crow, rain dove, kow-kow (for call)

COLAPTES: A noun coined from Greek *kolaptein* = to cut, chisel, peck at + suffix *-tēs* = agent, one that does. "Chipper" pertains to the technique used in nest construction and in the search for food. WOODPECKER FAMILY.

auratus: This Latin word for "ornamented with gold, gilded, golden" refers to the yellow color of the underwing. The red-shafted (*cafer*) group is now included in this species.

COMMON NAME: Northern Flicker for its summer range in the United States and Canada

OTHER NAMES: yellow-shafted woodpecker, high-hole, yarrup (for call)

COLINUS: A latinized form of Spanish *colin* from Nahuatl (Aztec) *zolin* = partridge, quail. QUAIL FAMILY.

virginianus: Coined Latin adjective for "Virginia" + suffix *-anus* = of or from. "Of Virginia" refers to the region where the type specimen was collected.

COMMON NAME: Northern Bobwhite for its range north of that of other quail species in Mexico and Central America; an onomatopoetic name for its call

OTHER NAMES: quail, partridge

COLUMBA: Latin word for "dove, pigeon." DOVE FAMILY.

livia: Postclassical Latin for "blue, leaden" (from *livēre* = to be black and blue, livid), which describes the reddish-blue plumage, although colors may vary

COMMON NAME: Rock Pigeon for the nesting habitat of the ancestral species on rocky cliffs

OTHER NAMES: rock dove, street pigeon, squab pigeon

CONTOPUS: From Greek *kontos* = short + *pous* = foot. "Short-footed" pertains to the relatively short "legs" (tarsi) of this genus. It is possible that the field observer could miss this anatomical feature. FLYCATCHER FAMILY.

cooperi: A latinized form of "Cooper's." This bird was named for William Cooper (1798–1864), an American conchologist, naturalist, and collector.

COMMON NAME: Olive-sided Flycatcher for the brownish-olive "vest" on the breast and sides

OTHER NAME: Nuttall's pewee

sordidulus: The Latin word for "rather soiled, smudged" describes the plumage of this species, which is generally darker and grayer than that of *C. virens.*

COMMON NAME: Western Wood-Pewee for its range and habitat

OTHER NAMES: large-billed wood-pewee, western pewee

virens: From a form of the Latin *virēre* = to be green. "Being green" refers to the generally greenish plumage.

COMMON NAME: Eastern Wood-Pewee for its range and habitat

OTHER NAMES: pewee flycatcher, pewit

CORAGYPS: From Greek *korax* = raven, crow + *gyps* = vulture. "Raven vulture" alludes to the black head and plumage. VULTURE FAMILY.

atratus: The Latin word for "clothed in black" addresses the color of the head and plumage of this bird.

COMMON NAME: Black Vulture

OTHER NAMES: black buzzard, black scavenger

CORVUS: The Latin word for "raven" (Greek *korax* = raven or crow). CROW FAMILY.

brachyrhynchos: From Greek *brachys* = short, little + *rhynchos* = beak, bill. "Small beak" is a comparative reference to a bill that is shorter and smaller than the large, heavy, curved beak of the raven.

COMMON NAME: American Crow to distinguish this native bird from the many Eurasian species

OTHER NAMES: common crow, corn-thief, caw

corax: From Greek *korax* = raven or crow. Another overnamed bird.

COMMON NAME: Common Raven for a species most frequently seen in the western and northern United States

OTHER NAMES: northern raven, American raven

cryptoleucus: From Greek *kryptos* = secret, hidden + *leukos* = white. "Hidden white" alludes to the white-based neck feathers, which are concealed, except when fluffed in display or ruffled in flight or by the wind.

COMMON NAME: Chihuahuan Raven for the range and habitat in southwestern deserts of open scrub and grasslands

OTHER NAME: white-necked raven

ossifragus: From Latin *os, ossis* (genitive) = bone + *frangere* = to break. "Bone breaker" describes this bird, which breaks open the shells of mollusks and crustaceans on which it feeds along beaches, marshes, swamps, and waterways.

COMMON NAME: Fish Crow for a diet that also includes marine carrion

OTHER NAMES: None found

COTURNICOPS: From Latin *coturnix, coturnicis* (genitive) = quail + Greek *ōps* = eye, face, appearance. "Quail-like" points out some similarity to quail in size and color. RAIL FAMILY.

noveboracensis: From Latin *novus* = new + *Eboracum*, the Roman name for the city of York in England + suffix -*ensis* = of or from a place. "Of New York" identifies where the type specimen was collected.

COMMON NAME: Yellow Rail for the buffy stripes on the back, paler on the underparts, and for the yellow bill of breeding birds

OTHER NAMES: clicker, water sparrow, yellow crake

CYANOCITTA: From Greek *kyaneos* = blue + *kitta/kissa* = a chattering bird, jay. "Blue chatterer" refers to the bright blue plumage of the head, nape, back, and tail of birds in this genus, whose calls can be loud, persistent, and varied. JAY FAMILY.

cristata: The Latin word for "crested, tufted" refers to the prominent blue crest.

COMMON NAME: Blue Jay

OTHER NAMES: common jay, jay-bird, nest robber, blue coat

stelleri: The Latin word for "Steller's." This bird is named for Georg Wilhelm Steller (1709–1746), a German naturalist. As a member of Vitus Bering's ill-fated second Kamchatka Expedition (1741–1742), Steller first described this bird, later known as Steller's Jay.

COMMON NAME: Steller's Jay

OTHER NAMES: mountain jay, conifer jay, black-headed jay

CYGNUS: The Latin word for "swan" (Greek *kyknos*). SWAN FAMILY.

buccinator: The Latin word for "trumpeter" describes this bird with its hollow, nasal, far-reaching honk.

COMMON NAME: Trumpeter Swan

OTHER NAME: bugler

columbianus: Coined Latin for "Columbia" + suffix *-anus* = of or from. "Of the Columbia" refers to the river in Oregon where the type specimen was collected.

COMMON NAME: Tundra Swan for its far-northern breeding range

OTHER NAMES: whistling swan, whistler

olor: A poetic Latin word for "swan [*cygnus*]."

COMMON NAME: Mute Swan is a misnomer—this swan hisses, snorts, and occasionally bugles.

OTHER NAMES: common swan, domestic swan

DENDROCYGNA: From Greek *dendron* = tree + Latin *cygnus* = swan. "Tree swan" is an inaccurate name for this genus of birds, which frequently perch and nest in trees, unlike swans—but they do have long necks. DUCK FAMILY.

autumnalis: Latin word for "of the autumn" explains when this species is often seen gleaning harvested fields.

COMMON NAME: Black-bellied Whistling-Duck for the black belly and a shrill whistle in flight

OTHER NAMES: tree duck, cornfield duck, red-billed whistling duck

bicolor: This Latin word for "two-colored" refers to the dominant plumage colors: orange-brown (face, neck, and belly) and black (back with chestnut barring).

COMMON NAME: Fulvous Whistling-Duck for the predominantly buffy or tawny plumage and a squeaky whistle when on the wing

OTHER NAMES: bicolored tree duck, long-legged duck, cornfield duck, squealer

DOLICHONYX: From Greek *dolichos* = long + *onyx* = claw. "Long claw" is an apt term for the very long "toes," which are ideal for perching in grasslands. BLACKBIRD FAMILY.

oryzivorus: From Greek and Latin *oryza* = rice + Latin *vorāre* = to eat greedily, devour. "Rice eater" describes well this species that consumes rice voraciously on its southward migration and on its wintering grounds in South America.

COMMON NAME: Bobolink, which is onomatopoetic

OTHER NAMES: rice bird, skunk bird, meadow-wink, bob-lincoln

DRYOCOPUS: From Greek *drys, dryos* (genitive) = oak tree, any timber tree + *kopis* = a cutter, cleaver or *kopos* = a striking, beating. Both words are related to *koptein* = to cut, peck at, hammer. "Tree striker" refers to the method of nest building and food gathering. WOODPECKER FAMILY.

pileatus: Latin for "wearing a felt cap [*pil(l)eus*]" alludes to the prominent red crest or "cap."

COMMON NAME: Pileated Woodpecker

OTHER NAMES: carpenter bird, great black woodpecker, cock-of-the-woods

DUMETELLA: From Latin *dumetum* = thicket, bramble + diminutive suffix *-ella.* "Little bramble(bird)" affirms the proclivity for dense thickets. MIMIC FAMILY.

carolinensis: Coined Latin adjective for "Carolina" + suffix *-ensis* = of or from a place. "Of the Carolina colonies" cites the region where the type specimen was obtained, in what is now Virginia.

COMMON NAME: Gray Catbird for the overall color and catlike calls between its whistles and other sounds

OTHER NAMES: black-capped thrush, slate-colored mockingbird, cat flycatcher

EGRETTA: A latinized form of "egret" from Old French *aigrette* = egret. HERON FAMILY.

caerulea: The Latin word for "blue" describes the plumage color of the adult.

COMMON NAME: Little Blue Heron for this wading bird, which is smaller than the Great Blue Heron (*Ardea herodias*)

OTHER NAMES: blue egret, blue crane, calico heron, little white crane (in immature plumage)

rufescens: A form of Latin *rufescere* = to become red, i.e., slightly red. "Reddish" is the color of the head and neck of the adult.

COMMON NAME: Reddish Egret

OTHER NAMES: plume bird, reddish heron

thula: According to some sources, *thula* is an Araucano (Chilean) name assigned to this species by Juan Ignacio Molina (1740–1829), Chilean priest and naturalist, in his *Saggio sulla Storia Naturale del Chili* (1782). Others suggest that Molina's *thula* is "Thule," which, according to ancient geographers and cartographers, was the unknown northernmost part of the world; the name, then, would be an allusion to the whiteness of the snow in that region.

COMMON NAME: Snowy Egret for the plumage "white as snow"

OTHER NAMES: golden slippers, little snowy, little white heron

tricolor: From the Latin prefix *tri-* = three + *color* = hue, tint. "Three color" describes the combination of slaty-blue upperparts, rusty neck, and white underparts.

COMMON NAME: Tricolored Heron

OTHER NAMES: Louisiana heron, lady-of-the-waters

ELANOIDES: From Greek *elanos* = kite + suffix *-oides* = similar to, resembling. "Resembling a kite"—which it is! HAWK FAMILY.

forficatus: From Latin *forfex, forficis* (genitive) = scissors, shears + suffix *-atus* = having, provided with. "Having a scissor(like) tail" refers to the long, forked tail.

COMMON NAME: Swallow-tailed Kite for the tail, which is deeply forked like that of some swallows

OTHER NAMES: fork-tailed kite, swallow-tailed hawk, snake hawk

ELANUS: A latinized form of the Greek word *elanos* = kite. HAWK FAMILY.

leucurus: From Greek *leukos* = white + *oura* = tail. "White tail" is descriptive of the tail and underparts.

COMMON NAME: White-tailed Kite

OTHER NAMES: black-shouldered kite, black-winged hawk, white hawk

EMPIDONAX: From Greek *empis, empidos* (genitive) = mosquito, gnat, small insect + *anax* = lord, master, king. "Lord of the insects" is an allusion to the dominating behavior and the main diet. FLYCATCHER FAMILY.

alnorum: From Latin *alnus* = alder tree. "Of the alders" applies to the habitat of these birds.

COMMON NAME: Alder Flycatcher

OTHER NAME: Traill's flycatcher (see *E. traillii*)

flaviventris: From Latin *flavus* = yellow, golden + *venter, ventris* (genitive) = belly. "Yellow belly" is a reference to the yellowish-olive underparts.

COMMON NAME: Yellow-bellied Flycatcher

OTHER NAMES: None found

hammondii: A latinized form of "Hammond's." This bird was named by John Xantus (1825–1894) for William Alexander Hammond (1828–1900), who became the surgeon general of the US Army. Like so many medical officers of this era, Hammond collected and prepared specimens for Spencer F. Baird. John Xantus, a Hungarian exile to the United States, was a social and professional charlatan but a gifted ornithologist and prolific collector of biota for Baird and others.

COMMON NAME: Hammond's Flycatcher

OTHER NAMES: None found

minimus: The Latin word for "smallest, least" indicates the size of this species, the smallest of this genus in the Upper Midwest.

COMMON NAME: Least Flycatcher

OTHER NAMES: chebec, sewick (for call)

oberholseri: A latinized form of "Oberholser's." This species was named for Harry Church Oberholser (1870–1963), an American ornithologist who was a senior biologist in the US Fish and Wildlife Service for many years and, later, curator of ornithology at the Cleveland Museum of Natural History. His most important contributions were in taxonomy; he named many new families, genera, and species. He also wrote the magisterial *The Bird Life of Texas*, published posthumously in 1974. Oberholser, active for 70 years in this field, also did important work in bird migration, banding, and censuses.

COMMON NAME: Dusky Flycatcher for the overall dark plumage

OTHER NAME: Wright's flycatcher

occidentalis: The Latin word for "western, westerly" refers to the range of this species in the western United States.

COMMON NAME: Cordilleran Flycatcher for its range among the western mountain chains

OTHER NAMES: None found

traillii: A latinized form of "Traill's." Thomas Stewart Traill (1781–1862) was a Scottish-born physician, naturalist, professor of medical jurisprudence, and supporter of Audubon, who named this bird for him.

COMMON NAME: Willow Flycatcher for its nesting habitat. At one time, the Willow and Alder Flycatchers were considered one species—Traill's Flycatcher.

OTHER NAME: little flycatcher

virescens: From a form of Latin *virescere* = to become green, i.e., slightly green. "Greenish" describes the olive-green back and head.

COMMON NAME: Acadian Flycatcher is perhaps a misnomer, since this species is not regularly found in the Maritime Provinces (Acadia). It is, however, "casual" in New Brunswick.

OTHER NAMES: green-crested flycatcher, small pewee

wrightii: A latinized form of "Wright's." This species was named for Charles Wright (1811–1885), a prolific collector of botanical specimens in the nineteenth century while traveling to the Southwest, Mexico, Cuba, Alaska, and abroad. He also collected many bird specimens, which he sent to Spencer F. Baird.

COMMON NAME: Gray Flycatcher for the overall gray plumage

OTHER NAME: Wright's flycatcher

EREMOPHILA: From Greek *erēmos* = desert, wilderness + *phila* = friendly with, loving. "Fond of open space" refers to habitat and nesting areas having low vegetation, such as fields, prairies, and tundra. LARK FAMILY.

alpestris: From Latin *alpes* = alps, high mountains + suffix *-tris* = belonging to, place where. "Of the mountains" indicates that some groups breed in the alpine life zone.

COMMON NAME: Horned Lark for the small feathered tufts ("horns") on the crown

OTHER NAMES: prairie bird, road lark, winter horned lark

EUDOCIMUS: A latinized form of the Greek *eudokimos* = in good repute, honored, famous, glorious. The application of this word is unclear. It may simply mean "glorious" for the brilliant all-white plumage. Joel Ellis Holloway, however, suggests that "in good repute" refers to the fact that Johann Georg Wagler (1800–1832), a German herpetologist and naturalist, removed this bird from the genus *Scolopax* and placed it in a new genus, thus establishing its "good standing" as a separate genus. IBIS FAMILY.

albus: The Latin word for "white" highlights the all-white plumage.

COMMON NAME: White Ibis

OTHER NAMES: white curlew, brown curlew, stone curlew

EUPHAGUS: From Greek prefix *eu-* = well, good + *phagos* = glutton. "Good eater" implies the vast variety of diet. BLACKBIRD FAMILY.

carolinus: A latinized adjective form of "Carolina" for the region where the type specimen was collected.

COMMON NAME: Rusty Blackbird for the rust-brown winter plumage of both male and female

OTHER NAMES: rusty grackle, rusty crow, marsh blackbird

cyanocephalus: From Latin *cyaneus* (Greek *kyaneos*) = blue, dark blue + Greek *kephalē* = the head. "Dark blue head" is a description of the glossy purple head and neck of the summer male.

COMMON NAME: Brewer's Blackbird, named for Thomas M. Brewer

OTHER NAMES: glossy blackbird, satin bird

FALCIPENNIS: From Latin *falx, falcis* (genitive) = sickle, scythe, pruning hook + *penna* = feather. "With sickle-shaped feathers" is an allusion to the unusually formed primary feathers. GROUSE FAMILY.

canadensis: Coined Latin adjective for "Canada" + suffix *-ensis* = of or from a place. "Canadian" refers to the range and region of the type specimen.

COMMON NAME: Spruce Grouse for the preferred habitat in coniferous forests and for its diet of spruce and fir buds and needles

OTHER NAMES: black grouse, pine grouse, fool hen, spotted grouse

FALCO: A postclassical Latin word for "falcon," from *falx, falcis* (genitive) = sickle, scythe, pruning hook. The allusion is to the curved talons and beak—or to the wings in flight. FALCON FAMILY.

columbarius: The Latin word for "pertaining to a pigeon or dove [*columba*]" refers to a frequent prey of this species.

COMMON NAME: Merlin. A form of this name for a small, strong falcon, known for centuries in Europe, occurs in many languages, e.g., *esmerillon* (Old French); *smirl* (Old High

German); *merlion* (Old English). The word developed through the ages to the modern *émerillon* (French); *Schmerl* (German); Merlin (English). The root *mer/mir*, common to all, seems to be traceable to the Greek *smyris* = (black) emery powder and to the Latin *merula* = black bird.

All of these names appear to account for the predominantly dark plumage of this bird. In the United States, the Pacific population is black; the taiga and prairie populations are progressively lighter. The same color variations occur in the Eurasian Merlin.

OTHER NAMES: pigeon hawk, little corporal

mexicanus: Coined Latin adjective for "Mexico" + suffix *-anus* = of or from. "Of Mexico" pertains to the locality of the type specimen taken at Monterrey, Nuevo León.

COMMON NAME: Prairie Falcon for the preferred habitat

OTHER NAME: bullet hawk

peregrinus: Latin for "foreign, of foreign places" from *peregrināri* = to travel about. "Wandering" is an appropriate adjective for this far-ranging bird, one of the most widely distributed in the world.

COMMON NAME: Peregrine Falcon

OTHER NAMES: duck hawk, wandering falcon, rock peregrine

rusticolus: The postclassical Latin word for "an inhabitant of the countryside" is a reference to the remote tundra habitat.

COMMON NAME: Gyrfalcon. The derivation of *gyr* is obscure. Some sources trace the word to *ger* = spear (German); *gyr(āri)* = to circle (Latin); *heiros* = sacred (Greek); *verthr* = worthy (Old Norse). The most accepted etymology seems to be *gir* = vulture (Old High German). The modern German word for vulture is the similar *Geier*, which gives credence to the Old High German source.

OTHER NAMES: winter hawk, partridge hawk, ice falcon, Greenland falcon

sparverius: The postclassical Latin word for "sparrow hawk" indicates its favorite prey.

COMMON NAME: American Kestrel distinguishes this bird from its Eurasian counterpart (*F. tinnunculus*). The word *kestrel* comes from Middle French *cresserelle* (Modern French *crecerelle*), "a kind of falcon." The word has its origin in Latin *crepitaculum*, "a noisy bell or rattle" (from *crepitāre* = to crackle, rattle), and is possibly named for the old belief that the rapid, high-pitched calls of this bird frightened other raptors away.

OTHER NAMES: sparrow hawk, windhover, killy hawk, cleek-cleek

FREGATA: A postclassical Latin word from Middle French *fregate* and Italian *fregata*, both meaning "a light war vessel, frigate," which pertains to the swift, nimble flight, similar to the movement of a frigate at sea. FRIGATEBIRD FAMILY.

magnificens: Latin word for "magnificent, distinguished, grand, noble." Although the Latin word bears no meaning of size or dimension, most sources consider this species "magnificent" because of its large size. A more accurate translation of *magnificens* is "impressive, splendid, fond of show," which would refer to the agile, skillful flight and dominating presence of this bird. Another meaning of *magnificens* is an ironic one, since the Latin can also mean "boastful, bragging," which could apply to the frigatebird's brazen and arrogant behavior of pirating prey from other birds. Irony and sarcasm, however, rarely occur in scientific nomenclature.

COMMON NAME: Magnificent Frigatebird

OTHER NAMES: man-o'-war, scissors-tail, hurricane bird, weather bird

FULICA: From Latin *fulix, fulicis* (genitive) = coot, a water-fowl. RAIL FAMILY.

americana: A latinized form of "American" to distinguish this species from the Eurasian coot (*F. atra*).

COMMON NAME: American Coot

OTHER NAMES: mud-hen, water chicken, pond crow, splatterer

GALLINAGO: From Latin *gallina* = hen + suffix *-ago* = having the character of, resembling. "Henlike" describes the small size and brown color and perhaps the "pecking" behavior. SNIPE FAMILY.

delicata: The Latin word for "dainty, charming" alludes to the small, pleasing appearance of this species.

COMMON NAME: Wilson's Snipe, named for Alexander Wilson

OTHER NAMES: common snipe, bog snipe, jacksnipe

GALLINULA: From Latin *gallina* = hen + diminutive suffix *-ula*. "Little chicken" expresses the similarity in appearance to a small domestic chicken. RAIL FAMILY.

galeata: The Latin word for "helmeted" (*galea* = helmet) implies the resemblance of the frontal shield to a helmet.

COMMON NAME: Common Gallinule for this species, which can be seen frequently within its range

OTHER NAMES: moorhen, water chicken

GAVIA: Latin word for "seabird." LOON FAMILY.

adamsii: A latinized form of "Adams's." This species is named for Edward Adams (1824–1856), a British naval surgeon who participated in several expeditions to Alaska and Canada in search of the Northwest Passage, and Sir John Franklin, who had disappeared on a previous expedition. A pioneer ornithologist in Alaska, Adams and others aboard the HMS *Enterprise* collected many bird species between 1850 and 1855 for the British Museum.

COMMON NAME: Yellow-billed Loon for the large yellow beak of breeding adults

OTHER NAMES: Adams's loon, white-billed loon

immer: The meaning of this term is uncertain. The species was named in 1764 by Morton Brünnich (1737–1827), a Danish naturalist who, it is assumed, was familiar with the local names for loon. On the northern coasts and islands of Scotland and Scandinavia, these local names varied: for example, *immer, imber, emmer, ymmer, hymber.* In the Shetlands, it was called the "immer goose." The Scandinavian word *immer* or *emmer,* meaning "ember(s)," the word for "blackened remains of a fire," was used to describe the dark plumage of breeding adults and ultimately became the name for the bird itself. Thomas Pennant (1726–1798), a Welsh zoologist, listed the bird as "Imber" in his *British Zoology* (1761–1766) and his *Genera of Birds* (1773). Sir Robert Sibbald (1641–1722), a Scottish physician, called it "Ember Goose" in his *Scotia Illustrata,* published in 1684. Other etymologies have been proposed for *immer,* such as Old Norse *himbrin* = loon; Latin *imbris* = rain; Latin *immergere* = to dive. While these suggestions have possible merit, the binomial *Gavia immer* most likely means "a black or dark (sea)bird."

COMMON NAME: Common Loon for a bird that nests across the northern lake country of the United States and Canada and is common in migration

OTHER NAMES: great northern diver, black-billed loon, ring-necked loon

pacifica: The postclassical Latin word for "pertaining to the Pacific Ocean" describes the range of this species along the Pacific coast of the United States and Canada.

COMMON NAME: Pacific Loon

OTHER NAME: Pacific diver

stellata: Latin word for "set with stars, starred," which refers to the sprinkling of white spots across the black back in winter plumage.

COMMON NAME: Red-throated Loon for the prominent red throat in breeding plumage

OTHER NAMES: red-throated diver, rain goose, little loon

GEOCOCCYX: From Greek *gē* = earth, land + *kokkyx* = the cuckoo. "Land cuckoo" refers to the tendency to spend much time on the ground. CUCKOO FAMILY.

californianus: Coined Latin adjective for "California" + suffix *-anus* = of or from. "Of California" designates the location of the type specimen.

COMMON NAME: Greater Roadrunner, which is larger than its Mexican counterpart (*G. velox*) and is frequently seen coursing along roads and through desert scrub and open brushland

OTHER NAMES: chaparral cock, lizard bird, paisano

GEOTHLYPIS: From Greek *gē* = land, earth + *thlypis* = a small, finchlike, seed-eating bird. This word is a variant reading of Aristotle's *thraupis*—a misnomer in either case for a warbler that is mostly insectivorous. "Earth bird" describes a species that is usually found close to the ground. WARBLER FAMILY.

formosa: The Latin word for "beautiful, handsome" emphasizes this bird's striking appearance.

COMMON NAME: Kentucky Warbler, which indicates where the type specimen was collected

OTHER NAME: Kentucky wagtail

philadelphia: A latinized adjective for "Philadelphia." The type specimen was taken within a few miles of this Pennsylvania city.

COMMON NAME: Mourning Warbler, whose dark gray head and breast with a black bib suggest "mourning attire"

OTHER NAMES: black-throated ground warbler, crape warbler, Philadelphia warbler

tolmiei: A latinized form of "Tolmie's." Dr. William Fraser Tolmie (1818–1886) was a Scot who worked as a chief factor for the Hudson Bay Company in Canada, where he became a well-known ornithologist.

COMMON NAME: MacGillivray's Warbler. The story of how this American bird got its name involves one warbler and four men. This bird was first named by John Kirk Townsend (see *Myadestes townsendi*) for his friend and colleague William Tolmie. In his *Narrative of a Journey across the Rocky Mountains to the Columbia River and a Visit to the Sandwich Islands, Chili, &c.* (1839), Townsend named the bird *Sylvia tolmiei* (Tolmie's Warbler). Soon after this, in the fifth volume of his 36-volume *Ornithological Biography* (1831–1839) and based on a skin of this species that he had obtained from Townsend, Audubon named the bird *Sylvia macgillivrayi* (MacGillivray's Warbler) for his friend and colleague. William MacGillivray (1796–1852) was a Scottish ornithologist and naturalist who had never set foot in America. Because Townsend's scientific name *tolmiei* was properly published first, it is retained by the Law of Priority. MacGillivray is retained in the common name. Both men are thus honored by a resolution worthy of Solomon.

OTHER NAMES: Tolmie's warbler, northern MacGillivray's warbler

trichas: A Greek word used by Aristotle for "a thrush with a shrill song," similar to that of this species.

COMMON NAME: Common Yellowthroat for a species widespread in the continental United States and most of Canada whose throat below the dark mask is bright yellow

OTHER NAMES: Maryland yellow-throat, black-masked ground warbler, domino bird, bandit

GRUS: The Latin word for "crane." CRANE FAMILY.

americana: A latinized adjective form of "America" identifies the North American range of this bird.

COMMON NAME: Whooping Crane for the loud, resonant, bugling call of this marsh-dwelling bird

OTHER NAMES: whooper, great white crane, garoo (for call)

canadensis: Coined Latin adjective for "Canada" + the suffix *-ensis* = of or from a place. "Canadian" refers to the locality of the type specimen taken in Hudson Bay and to the breeding range of this bird.

COMMON NAME: Sandhill Crane for the spring staging grounds in the Sand Hills of south-central Nebraska

OTHER NAMES: field crane, baldhead, upland crane

GYMNORHINUS: From Greek *gymnos* = naked, bare, unclad + *rhis, rhinos* (genitive) = nose. "Bare nose" refers to the nostrils, which are not covered with feathers, unlike those of most corvids. JAY FAMILY.

cyanocephalus: From Greek *kyaneos* = (dark) blue + *kephalē* = the head. "Blue-headed" refers especially to the head feathers, which are bluer than the other plumage feathers of adult birds.

COMMON NAME: Pinyon Jay, which pertains to feeding areas of pinyon, juniper, and oak in the foothills and higher altitudes of the western United States

OTHER NAMES: blue crow, pine jay, piñonero, Maximilian's jay (for Maximilian, Prince of Wied, a noted nineteenth-century German traveler in the American West, who discovered and named this bird)

HAEMORHOUS: From Greek *haima* = blood; also a reddish, purplish dye obtained from the root of the *anxousa* = the plant *Anchusa tinctoria* (alkanet) + *rhoous/rhous* = a stream, a current, a pouring. "Washed in red" describes the varying hues on the head, breast, and rump of birds in this genus. FINCH FAMILY.

cassinii: A latinized form of "Cassin's." This bird was named for John Cassin.

COMMON NAME: Cassin's Finch

OTHER NAME: Cassin's purple finch

mexicanus: Coined Latin adjective for "Mexico" + suffix *-anus* = of or from. "Of Mexico" refers to the region where the type specimen was collected.

COMMON NAME: House Finch for its affinity with human dwellings

OTHER NAMES: crimson-fronted finch, redhead, Mexican house finch

purpureus: The Latin word for "purple" describes the raspberry-colored head, breast, and rump of the adult male.

COMMON NAME: Purple Finch

OTHER NAMES: eastern purple finch, purple grosbeak

HALIAEETUS: From Greek *hals, halos* (genitive) = salt, sea + *aetos* = eagle. "Sea eagle" pertains to the breeding and feeding areas along coasts, lakes, and rivers. HAWK FAMILY.

leucocephalus: From Greek *leukos* = white, bright + *kephalē* = the head. "White-headed" refers to the feathers on the head of the mature bird.

COMMON NAME: Bald Eagle, an uncommon use of the word *bald*, which here means "marked with white"

OTHER NAMES: white-headed sea eagle, fish eagle, black eagle

HELMITHEROS: From the Greek *helmis* = little worm + *thēran* = to hunt, chase. "Worm hunter" is an apparent misnomer, since this species is mostly insectivorous; it does, however, eat smooth caterpillars. WARBLER FAMILY.

vermivorum: Latin *vermis* = worm + *vorāre* = to eat. "Worm eating" is another misnomer.

COMMON NAME: Worm-eating Warbler

OTHER NAMES: worm-eater, worm-eating swamp warbler

HIMANTOPUS: From Greek *himas, himantos* (genitive) = leather thong or strap + *pous* = foot. Literally "strapfoot," this word is used for a wading bird with legs as long and narrow as a leather thong (see *Calidris himantopus*). STILT FAMILY.

mexicanus: Coined Latin adjective for "Mexico" + suffix *-anus* = of or from. "Of Mexico" indicates where the type specimen was collected.

COMMON NAME: Black-necked Stilt for the distinctive black markings on the neck and head

OTHER NAMES: longshanks, lawyer, daddy longlegs

HIRUNDO: The Latin word for "a swallow." SWALLOW FAMILY.

rustica: Latin for "of or in the country, rustic." This species is usually seen on farmland in the countryside.

COMMON NAME: Barn Swallow for nesting sites on or in barns and other buildings

OTHER NAMES: common swallow, eave swallow, forked-tailed swallow

HISTRIONICUS: Latin for "of or pertaining to an actor [*histrio*]." The translation "histrionic" captures the dramatic plumage and pattern of dots and streaks, which resemble the costume of a harlequin. DUCK FAMILY.

histrionicus: A tautonym.

COMMON NAME: Harlequin Duck for the variegated colors and pattern

OTHER NAMES: painted duck, lord-and-lady, circus duck

HYDROCOLOEUS: From Greek *hydor* = water + *koloios* = jackdaw. "Water daw" implies the similarity of this gull to the Daurian Jackdaw (*Corvus dauuricus*). Both birds range from Eastern Europe to parts of Asia, are approximately the same size, and have similar plumage patterns: black head, dark under-wings, and light body. GULL FAMILY.

minutus: The Latin word for "small, little" refers to the size.

COMMON NAME: Little Gull, the smallest of all gulls

OTHER NAMES: None found

HYDROPROGNE: From Greek *hydor* = water + Progne (also Procne), a woman in a gory Greek myth who was turned into a swallow (Ovid). "Water swallow" is an apt description of this bird's swallowlike flight over water. TERN FAMILY.

caspia: Latin form of "Caspian" for the location of the type specimen taken on the Caspian Sea.

COMMON NAME: Caspian Tern

OTHER NAMES: redbill, imperial tern

HYLOCICHLA: From Greek *hylē* = woodland, forest + *kichlē* = a thrush. "Wood thrush" aptly describes the preferred deep-woods habitat. THRUSH FAMILY.

mustelina: Latin for "of a weasel [*mustela*]." The allusion is to the brown face and white underparts of both bird and mammal.

COMMON NAME: Wood Thrush

OTHER NAMES: song thrush, wood robin, flute

ICTERIA: From Greek *ikteros* = jaundice; also a bird with yellowish-green plumage. According to Greek myth, a jaundiced person was cured by seeing this bird, whereupon the bird, alas, would die. WARBLER FAMILY.

virens: A form of Latin *virēre* = to be green. "Being green" refers to the olive-green upperparts.

COMMON NAME: Yellow-breasted Chat for the yellow breast and many varied songs, calls, trills, and rattles

OTHER NAMES: yellow mockingbird, polyglot chat, long-tailed chat

ICTERUS: The postclassical Latin word for "yellow" (Greek *ikteros*) applies to the shades of yellow that appear on many species of this genus. ORIOLE FAMILY.

bullockii: A latinized form of "Bullock's." This species was named for William Bullock (ca. 1773–1849), a British traveler, archaeologist, land speculator, naturalist, and bird collector. With his son, also named William, Bullock collected many birds in Mexico in the 1820s, including the type specimen of this species. When Swainson named this species, he probably had both Bullocks in mind.

COMMON NAME: Bullock's Oriole

OTHER NAMES: None found

galbula: Diminutive of Latin *galbina* = a small yellow bird; both words are forms of *galgulus* = a small bird (Pliny). "Little yellow bird" refers to the variable orange plumage of the underparts and outer tail feathers of both the male and female.

COMMON NAME: Baltimore Oriole, named for the Calverts, lords of Baltimore, whose coat of arms includes the colors yellow and black

OTHER NAMES: hang-nest, firebird, hammock-bird

spurius: Latin word for "of illegitimate birth." Because of its color, the female of this species was first thought to be a first-year male *I. galbula* and, therefore, was named Bastard Baltimore Oriole. When the confusion was resolved, the common name was changed. The specific *spurius* is retained by the Law of Priority.

COMMON NAME: Orchard Oriole for its frequent use of this habitat

OTHER NAMES: brown oriole, basket-bird, swinger

ICTINIA: From Greek *iktinos* = a kite. HAWK FAMILY.

mississippiensis: Coined Latin adjective for "Mississippi" + suffix *-ensis* = of or from a place. "Of Mississippi" identifies the locality of the type specimen taken near Natchez, Mississippi.

COMMON NAME: Mississippi Kite

OTHER NAMES: blue kite, Louisiana kite, locust-eater

IXOBRYCHUS: From Greek *ixos* = mistletoe + *brychein* = to eat, devour. "Mistletoe eater" is a misnomer. Gustav Johan Billberg (1772–1844), a Swedish botanist and zoologist, may have confused both words: *ixos* with *ixias* = an aquatic reedlike plant; and *brychein* with, possibly, *bebrycha*, a form of the verb *brychasthai* = to roar or bellow. Billberg's apparent intent was to create the name "reed roarer," thus accommodating the folk belief that bitterns blow into a reed to produce their loud, booming sounds. Here, too, Billberg missed the mark: the cooing, clucking calls of birds in this genus are hardly "booming." HERON FAMILY. (Note: It is interesting that Ixobrychus is the name of the ornithological association of Slovenia [OAI].)

exilis: This Latin word for "small, slender" refers to size.

COMMON NAME: Least Bittern, one of the smallest herons

OTHER NAMES: little heron, dwarf bittern

IXOREUS: From Greek *ixos* = mistletoe (berry) + *oros, oreos* (genitive) = mountain, hill. "Mountain berry (eater)": the berry here is that of the mistletoe, which parasitizes several species of juniper in the Rocky Mountains and the Northwest. This monotype also eats insects, snowberries, blackberries, raspberries, and the berries of the toxic poison oak. Ernest A. Choate notes that "the plant [*ixos*] has been associated from the time of Aristotle with a European thrush which breeds in the mountains." The moist forests and mountain lakes at higher altitudes are the preferred habitat of this genus. THRUSH FAMILY.

naevius: Latin for "having a mole or birthmark on the body," an apparent reference to the multipatterned and variegated plumage.

COMMON NAME: Varied Thrush

OTHER NAMES: Oregon robin, Alaska robin, northern varied thrush

JUNCO: From Latin *juncus* = a rush. "Of the rushes" is an odd name, since this bird is associated with northern forests, woodlands, hedges, and shrubs. SPARROW FAMILY.

hyemalis: A form of the Latin *hiemalis*, meaning "of the winter," is a reference to the northern breeding range. The *hyemalis* group arrives in the Upper Midwest in late fall and early winter.

COMMON NAME: Dark-eyed Junco, which distinguishes those groups with dark eyes (Slate-colored, Oregon, Gray-headed, Pink-sided, White-winged) from the western Yellow-eyed Junco (*J. phaeonotus*)

OTHER NAMES: snowbird, white-bill, black chipping bird

LANIUS: The Latin word for "butcher, exterminator" confirms the practice of impaling prey on thorns, barbed wire, or sharp twigs. SHRIKE FAMILY.

excubitor: Latin word for "one who keeps watch, a sentinel." Linnaeus gives this reason for choosing the specific name: "Accipitres adventates observat et aviculis indicat" (It watches for approaching hawks and points them out to small birds). An odd name; an odder explanation.

COMMON NAME: Northern Shrike for its breeding range in the United States

OTHER NAMES: butcher bird, nine-killer, Devil's bird

ludovicianus: A postclassical Latin adjective for *Ludovicus* (Louis XIV), meaning "of Louisiana (Territory)," where the type specimen was collected.

COMMON NAME: Loggerhead Shrike for the disproportionately large head

OTHER NAMES: butcher bird, cotton picker

LARUS: Latin *larus* and Greek *laros* = voracious seabird, gull. GULL FAMILY.

argentatus: Latin word for "ornamented with silver [*argentum*]," which here means silver-colored. "Silvery" reflects the pale gray back and wings of the adult.

COMMON NAME: Herring Gull for the consumption of fish, a small part of the diet of this omnivorous bird

OTHER NAMES: Common gull, harbor gull, lake gull, winter gull

californicus: A coined Latin adjective for "California" + suffix *-icus* = of or pertaining to. "Of California" identifies the location of the type specimen.

COMMON NAME: California Gull

OTHER NAMES: None found

canus: The Latin word for "gray, hoary," which describes the medium-gray back and wings of the adult.

COMMON NAME: Mew Gull. According to some sources, the name is imitative of the call, but the name may be a later form of the Old English *mæw* (German *Möwe*), meaning "gull."

OTHER NAMES: sea mew, short-billed gull

delawarensis: Coined Latin adjective for "Delaware" + suffix *-ensis* = of or from a place. "From Delaware" cites the location of the type specimen taken on the Delaware River near Philadelphia, Pennsylvania.

COMMON NAME: Ring-billed Gull for the broad dark band near the tip of the yellow bill

OTHER NAMES: pond gull, squeaky gull

fuscus: The Latin word for "dark, dusky" refers to the dark gray back and wings of the adult plumage.

COMMON NAME: Lesser Black-backed Gull for a species that is much smaller than the Great Black-backed Gull (*L. marinus*)

OTHER NAMES: None found

glaucescens: A form of the inferred Latin verb *glaucescere* (Latin *glaucus*, Greek *glaukos*) = to become gray, i.e., slightly gray. "Grayish" describes the pale gray back and wings of the adult plumage.

COMMON NAME: Glaucous-winged Gull for the pale gray wings

OTHER NAMES: None found

glaucoides: From Greek *glaukos* (Latin *glaucus*) = gray + suffix *-oides* = similar to, resembling. "Like the Glaucous" points out the similarity to the Glaucous Gull (*L. hyperboreus*), which was formerly *L. glaucus*.

COMMON NAME: Iceland Gull for the location of the type specimen; however, this species does not breed in Iceland.

OTHER NAME: white-winged gull

hyperboreus: A latinized form of Greek *hyperboreas* = beyond the north wind (*Boreas*). "Far northern" is appropriate for the breeding range of this bird.

COMMON NAME: Glaucous Gull (formerly *L. glaucus*) for the pale gray (Latin *glaucus*, Greek *glaukos*) back and wings of the adult

OTHER NAMES: ice gull, owl gull, burgomaster gull

marinus: The Latin word for "of the sea, marine" alludes to the coastal ranges of this species.

COMMON NAME: Great Black-backed Gull for the dark gray back and wings of the adult; larger than the Lesser Black-backed Gull (*L. fuscus*) and one of the largest and darkest of gulls

OTHER NAMES: saddleback, black minister, coffin-carrier

schistisagus: From the Latin adjective *schistos* = split, separated, cleft; from Greek *schizein* = to split, cleave. The allusion here is to the color of split rock, such as slate or schist (metamorphic rocks) + *sagos* = cloak, mantle. "Slate-colored mantle" is a rather geological description of the back and wings of the adult.

COMMON NAME: Slaty-backed Gull

OTHER NAMES: None found

thayeri: A latinized form of "Thayer's." John Eliot Thayer (1862–1933) was an American patron of many ornithological expeditions. His extensive collection of ornithological realia was donated to the Louis Agassiz Museum of Comparative Zoology at Harvard University.

COMMON NAME: Thayer's Gull

OTHER NAMES: None found

LATERALLUS: From Latin *latēre* = to lie hidden or concealed, to keep out of sight + postclassical Latin *rallus* = rail. "Skulking rail" is a very apt name for this secretive genus. RAIL FAMILY.

jamaicensis: Coined Latin adjective for "Jamaica" + suffix *-ensis* = of or from a place. "Of Jamaica" refers to the locality of the type specimen.

COMMON NAME: Black Rail for the grayish-black plumage

OTHER NAMES: little black rail, black crake

LEUCOPHAEUS: From Greek *leukophaēs* = white, gleaming. "Shining white" reflects the summer plumage of the neck, tail, and underparts of adult birds in this genus. GULL FAMILY.

atricilla: From Latin *ater* = black + spurious Latin *cilla* = tail. "Black-tailed" refers to the broad dark tail band of first winter birds and those with juvenal plumage.

COMMON NAME: Laughing Gull, well named for the chuckling call

OTHER NAME: black-headed gull

pipixcan: This curious name is a Nahuatl (Aztec) word for a gull-like bird, first mentioned by Francisco Hernández de Toledo (1514–1587), a Spanish physician and naturalist, in his *Historia Avium Novae Hispaniae*, published in Rome in 1651. The bird was named and described as a new species (*Larus pipixcan* spec. nov.) by Johann Georg Wagler (1800–1832), a German herpetologist and naturalist, in Lorenz Oken's journal, *Isis* (vol. 24, 1831).

COMMON NAME: Franklin's Gull, named for Sir John Franklin (1786–1847), a British naval officer and Arctic explorer who perished while searching for the Northwest Passage

OTHER NAMES: Franklin's rosy gull, prairie pigeon, grasshopper gull

LEUCOSTICTE: From Greek *leukos* = white + *stiktos* = marked, spotted, dappled. "Palely flecked" refers to the pinkish-white mottling of the wings and underparts. FINCH FAMILY.

tephrocotis: From Greek *tephros* = the color of ashes (*tephra*), i.e., gray + *kot(t)is* = the head (a Doric dialect word for *kephalē*). "Gray head" is appropriate for the gray occiput of both the male and female.

COMMON NAME: Gray-crowned Rosy-Finch

OTHER NAMES: brown snow-bird, pink snow-bird

LIMNODROMUS: From Greek *limnē* = pond, marsh, standing water + *dromos* = a place in which to run (*dramein*), i.e., inhabiting. "Marsh dweller" describes the habitat and feeding area of birds in this genus. SANDPIPER FAMILY.

griseus: Postclassical Latin word meaning "gray, grizzled," which describes the color of the winter plumage.

COMMON NAME: Short-billed Dowitcher for the seemingly shorter bill than that of *L. scolopaceus*, although this distinction is not reliable. *Dowitcher* is an Iroquois word for this bird.

OTHER NAMES: gray-back, brown snipe, robin snipe, eastern dowitcher

scolopaceus: From Latin *scolopax* = woodcock + suffix *-eus* = having the quality of. The Greek *skolops*, meaning "anything pointed," e.g., for impaling, is an accurate word for the long, probing bill of this species. (Note: This is one of the few type specimens from the Upper Midwest. It was collected by Thomas Say at Boyer Creek near Council Bluffs, Iowa, in 1823.)

COMMON NAME: Long-billed Dowitcher for the seemingly longer bill than that of *L. griseus*. *Dowitcher* is an Iroquois word for this bird.

OTHER NAMES: greater long-beak, greater gray-back, red-bellied snipe, western dowitcher

LIMNOTHLYPIS: Greek *limnē* = pond, marsh, standing water + *thlypis* = a small, finchlike, seed-eating bird. This word is a variant reading of Aristotle's *thraupis*. In either case, this is a misnomer for a warbler that is mostly insectivorous. "Marsh bird" is well named, for it is frequently found near water. WARBLER FAMILY.

swainsonii: A latinized form of "Swainson's." Audubon named this species for his friend William Swainson.

COMMON NAME: Swainson's Warbler

OTHER NAMES: None found

LIMOSA: Latin adjective from *limus* = mud, mire + suffix *-osa* = full of. "Muddy" refers to the habitat sought in migration— mudflats, beaches, and edges of ponds. GODWIT FAMILY.

fedoa: A word of unknown origin and, apparently, lost in the mists of time. Some sources suggest that this word is a latinized form of an Old English word for "godwit" or an Italian dialect word for this bird. Coues gives other possibilities. We have another suggestion—the word may be a transposed form of the Latin verb *fodāre/fodere,* meaning "to dig, dig up, stab, pierce," all of which could describe the probing of the long bill while feeding.

COMMON NAME: Marbled Godwit for the dappled pattern of its plumage

OTHER NAMES: spike-bill, red curlew, great godwit

haemastica: From Greek *haimatikos* = pertaining to the blood (*haima*). One wonders how the *s* wandered into the word. "Blood-red" alludes to the dark reddish-brown breast and underparts of the breeding plumage.

COMMON NAME: Hudsonian Godwit for the location of the type specimen taken in Hudson Bay

OTHER NAMES: red-breasted godwit, little curlew, white rump

LOPHODYTES: From Greek *lophos* = crest, tuft on head + *dytēs* = diver. "Crested diver" is a good description of this genus. DUCK FAMILY.

cucullatus: Latin for "having a hood [*cucullus*]." The translation "hooded" captures the illusion of a cowl-like crest.

COMMON NAME: Hooded Merganser

OTHER NAMES: fan-crested duck, little sawbill, cottontop

LOXIA: From Greek *loxos* = slanting, crosswise. "Crossed" describes the unusual structure of the bill, crossed at the tips. FINCH FAMILY.

curvirostra: From Latin *curvus* = crooked, bent, curved + *rostrum* = bill, beak. "Crossed bills" is another reference to the offset structure of the upper and lower mandibles.

COMMON NAME: Red Crossbill for the reddish-orange plumage of the adult male

OTHER NAMES: American crossbill, common crossbill

leucoptera: From Greek *leukos* = white, pale + *pteron* = wing. "White wings" is a generous description for the two white wingbars.

COMMON NAME: White-winged Crossbill

OTHER NAMES: None found

MEGACERYLE: From Greek *megas* = large, great + *kērylos* = kingfisher, halcyon. "Large kingfisher" distinguishes this genus from the genera of smaller kingfishers. KINGFISHER FAMILY.

alcyon: Greek *alkyon* = kingfisher. The ancients distinguished the *alkyon* from the *kērylos*; this distinction has been lost. The *alkyon* appears in several forms: to the Greek poet Alcman, it is a "harbinger of spring"; the personified Alcyone is the brightest star in the constellation Pleiades; in Ovid's *Metamorphoses*, Alcyone (or Halcyone), daughter of Aeolus, ruler of the winds, throws herself into the sea where her husband, Ceyx, has drowned. Out of pity, Zeus changes them into kingfishers (*alkyones*). The kingfisher was thought to build a floating nest on the surface of the ocean at the time of the winter solstice when Aeolus calms the waters for 14 days—these are the "halcyon days."

COMMON NAME: Belted Kingfisher for the distinct blue-gray breast band of both male and female

OTHER NAMES: halcyon, blue diver, fly-up-the-creek

MEGASCOPS: From Greek *megas* = large + *skōps* = a small horned owl. "Large little owl" is an oxymoronic name that is not much help in identification. OWL FAMILY.

asio: Pliny's word for "a kind of horned owl." Coues suggests that *asio* is a Hebrew word but cites no source.

COMMON NAME: Eastern Screech-Owl for its range east of the Rocky Mountains and for its call, which is not a screech but rather a descending whinny or a soft, quavering yodel

OTHER NAMES: shivering owl, cat owl, red owl, gray owl

MELANERPES: From Greek *melas*, *melanos* (genitive) = black + *herpein* = to creep. "Black creeper" accounts for the color on the tail, back, and wings of birds in this genus and for their activity on trees. WOODPECKER FAMILY.

carolinus: A coined Latin adjective meaning "of the Carolinas" that refers to the region of the type specimen, which was obtained in South Carolina.

COMMON NAME: Red-bellied Woodpecker for the seldom seen pink or reddish wash on the belly

OTHER NAMES: zebra-back, cham-chack (for call)

erythrocephalus: From Greek *erythros* = red + *kephalē* = the head. "Red head" is the prominent feature of this otherwise black-and-white bird.

COMMON NAME: Red-headed Woodpecker

OTHER NAMES: tri-color, white shirt, flag bird

lewis: This bird was named by Alexander Wilson for Captain Meriwether Lewis (1774–1809), who collected the type specimen in Idaho while on the renowned Lewis and Clark Expedition.

COMMON NAME: Lewis's Woodpecker

OTHER NAMES: black woodpecker, crow woodpecker

MELANITTA: From Greek *melas, melanos* (genitive) = black, dark, dusky + *nētta* = a duck. The Law of Priority retains the misspelling of *nētta.* It is, however, possible that *itta* is a diminutive suffix; if so, *Melanitta* would mean "little black one." "Dark duck" applies to all the species in this genus, especially in breeding plumage. DUCK FAMILY.

americana: A coined Latin adjective for "American," which distinguishes this bird from the Eurasian species (*M. nigra*).

COMMON NAME: Black Scoter, which refers to the all-black plumage of the adult duck

OTHER NAMES: black butterbill, copper-nose, pumpkin-blossom coot

fusca: The Latin word for "dark, dusky" describes the general color in all plumages.

COMMON NAME: White-winged Scoter for the white patches on the dark wings, especially visible in flight

OTHER NAMES: velvet duck, black whistler, black white-wing

perspicillata: A postclassical Latin word that could have been coined from either the verb *perspicere* = to see through, or the adjective *perspicibilis* = bright, something easily seen. This neologism, therefore, has two possible meanings, both with merit: "something seen through," e.g., a lens, spectacles (verbal); or, as suggested by Coues, "something easily seen, conspicuous, spectacular" (adjectival). The translation "spectacled" refers to the black disks resembling spectacles (sunglasses?) on the large, colorful bill, while the equally appropriate translation "spectacular" describes the conspicuous, multicolored bill and striking white patches on the forehead and nape.

COMMON NAME: Surf Scoter for this diver, which is most at home in the surf on both coasts and the interior Great Lakes in winter

OTHER NAMES: spectacled coot, skunkhead, goggle-nose

MELEAGRIS: Greek word for "guinea-fowl." This genus is named for Meleager, a Greek hero, whose death his sisters mourned so pitifully that the goddess Diana turned them into guinea-fowl, according to Ovid. There are no native guinea-fowl in the Americas. According to the *Oxford English Dictionary*, guinea-fowl were imported from Africa through Turkey, hence the common name for a bird that resembled guinea-fowl. The name "turkie" or "turkey" has apparently been in use since the sixteenth century for guinea-fowl, peafowl, and turkeys. TURKEY FAMILY.

gallopavo: From Latin *gallus* = rooster, cock + *pavo* = peacock. "Peacock" likens the intricate patterns of the fanned tail of the strutting turkey to those of the peacock.

COMMON NAME: Wild Turkey for the undomesticated bird

OTHER NAMES: gobbler, wood turkey, American wild turkey

MELOSPIZA: From Greek *melos* = song + *spiza* = finch. "Song finch" refers to the varied musical trills and sweet tones of birds in this genus. SPARROW FAMILY.

georgiana: A latinized adjective form for "Georgia" + suffix -*ina* = of or from. "Of Georgia" identifies where the type specimen was collected.

COMMON NAME: Swamp Sparrow for its habitat

OTHER NAMES: swamp song sparrow, marsh sparrow, swamp finch

lincolnii: A latinized form of "Lincoln's." Audubon named this species for Thomas Lincoln (1812–1883), an important member of Audubon's Labrador Expedition in 1833.

COMMON NAME: Lincoln's Sparrow

OTHER NAMES: Lincoln's song sparrow, Tom's finch

melodia: This Latin word for "pleasant song, melody" describes the rich, modulated singing of this species.

COMMON NAME: Song Sparrow

OTHER NAMES: bush sparrow, silver tongue, everybody's darling

MERGUS: Latin word for "diver, a kind of waterfowl." DUCK FAMILY.

merganser: From Latin *mergere* = to dip, dive, immerse + *anser* = goose. "Diving goose" is an obvious misnomer for this diving duck.

COMMON NAME: Common Merganser for this species, which is widely distributed throughout the United States and Canada, except in the southeastern states

OTHER NAMES: goosander, fish duck, sawbill

serrator: Coined Latin word from *serra* = a saw + suffix *-tor* = agent, something that does. "Sawyer" refers to the use of the serrated bill.

COMMON NAME: Red-breasted Merganser for the dark red throat of the male in breeding plumage

OTHER NAMES: red-breasted goosander, little fish duck, sawbill

MIMUS: Latin word (Greek *mimos*) for "imitator, mime." MIMIC FAMILY.

polyglottos: From Greek *polys* = many + *glōtta* = tongue. "Multilingual" is an apt adjective for the versatile mimicry of this species.

COMMON NAME: Northern Mockingbird to distinguish this species from tropical mockingbirds and for its ability to imitate sounds

OTHER NAMES: mocker, mimic thrush, mock bird

MNIOTILTA: From Greek *mnion* = moss + *tillein* = to pluck, to pull out. "Moss plucker" describes the nest-building material and how it is obtained. WARBLER FAMILY.

varia: A Latin word for "variegated, striped," which refers to the markings of the plumage.

COMMON NAME: Black-and-white Warbler for colors of plumage

OTHER NAMES: whitepoll warbler, striped warbler, creeping warbler

MOLOTHRUS: The origin of this word is uncertain. Most sources consider it a misspelling of the Greek *molobros*, meaning "a greedy beggar," and by extension, "a vagabond, tramp." If so, the misspelling is retained by the Law of Priority. Coues, however, writes that Swainson, who named this genus and who knew his Latin, wrote the word *molothrus* and may have coined the word from Greek *mōlos*, meaning "a struggle, contest, quarrel," and a form of the verb *thrōskein*, meaning "to spring at, attack, rush, dart." That form, we suggest, may be the Greek *thouros*, meaning "rash, impetuous, hurried, presumptuous," which could easily have become *thrus* in a latinized transliteration. The result would be *molothrus*, i.e., "an impetuous, presumptuous struggle." Both *molobros* and *molothrus* seem to be appropriate appellations for this genus, which "wanders" from nest to nest and, with metaphorical impetuosity, lays its unwelcome eggs in the nests of other species. BLACKBIRD FAMILY.

ater: This Latin word for "black, dark" describes the body plumage of the adult male.

COMMON NAME: Brown-headed Cowbird for the coffee-colored head and neck of the adult male

OTHER NAMES: buffalo bird, little blackbird, lazy bird

MYADESTES: From Greek *myia* = a fly + *edestēs* = eater. "Fly eater" refers to the chief diet of this genus, consisting of insects, spiders, worms—and berries in winter. THRUSH FAMILY.

townsendi: A latinized form of "Townsend's." John Kirk Townsend (1809–1851) was a skilled and respected ornithologist from Philadelphia who catalogued the birds of the Oregon Territory in the appendix to his *Narrative of a Journey across the Rocky Mountains to the Columbia River and a Visit to the Sandwich Islands, Chili, &c.* (1839). Many think that Townsend's contribution to ornithology has not received the recognition it deserves.

COMMON NAME: Townsend's Solitaire for the shyness of this elusive species

OTHER NAME: fly-catching thrush

MYCTERIA: From Greek *myktēr* = nose, snout + suffix *-ia* = pertaining to. "Of the nose" is a modest description of the very large, long bill. STORK FAMILY.

americana: The postclassical Latin word for "of America" defines this bird's range in the Western Hemisphere.

COMMON NAME: Wood Stork, the only North American stork; it roosts in swampy, wooded areas and builds its platform nests in trees.

OTHER NAMES: wood ibis, gourdhead, preacher

MYIARCHUS: From Greek *myia* = a fly + *archōn* = chief, commander, ruler. "Lord of the flies" is an appropriate name for the behavior and diet of birds in this genus. FLYCATCHER FAMILY.

cinerascens: A form of the Latin *cinerescere* = to turn to ashes (*cineres*). "Ashy" refers to the pale gray throat and breast.

COMMON NAME: Ash-throated Flycatcher

OTHER NAMES: None found

crinitus: The Latin word for "having long hair, hairy" is in reference to the crest of this species.

COMMON NAME: Great Crested Flycatcher for the obvious crest and size

OTHER NAMES: greatcrest, May-bird, wheep (for call)

NUCIFRAGA: From Latin *nux*, *nucis* (genitive) = nut + *frangere* = to break. "Nut breaker" describes the method of procuring the preferred food of pinyon nuts, conifer seeds, and acorns. CROW FAMILY.

columbiana: A latinized adjective form for "Columbian." The type specimen was collected on the Clearwater River, a tributary of the Columbia, in Idaho.

COMMON NAME: Clark's Nutcracker, named for Captain William Clark (1770–1838), who collected the type specimen on the Lewis and Clark Expedition (1804–1806)

OTHER NAMES: gray crow, camp robber, woodpecker crow

NUMENIUS: A latinized form of the Greek *noumenios*, meaning "a kind of curlew." The Greek word is formed from *neos* = new + *mēnē* = moon + suffix *-ios* = pertaining to. "New moon bird" is named for the arcuate shape of the long, thin bill, which is likened to the crescent of the new moon. There is another etymological possibility for *Numenius*: the base word may be Latin *numen*, "a nodding with the head movement," which could describe the bird's feeding behavior. CURLEW FAMILY.

americanus: A coined latinized adjective form for "America" + suffix *-anus* = of or from. "Of America" identifies the breeding range in the western United States and distinguishes this species from other curlews in the world.

COMMON NAME: Long-billed Curlew for the longest bill of all curlews

OTHER NAMES: big curlew, sickle-bill, sabre-bill

phaeopus: From Greek *phaios* = dusky, gray + *pous* = foot. "Gray-footed" applies to the color of the feet and legs of the adult.

COMMON NAME: Whimbrel. This name apparently comes from the English word *whimper* (German *wimmern*) + the diminutive suffix *-el*, i.e., "a small whimperer." The name is onomatopoetic.

OTHER NAMES: short-billed curlew, Hudsonian curlew, striped-head

NYCTANASSA: From Greek *nyx, nyktos* (genitive) = night + *anassa* = queen, lady. "Queen of the night" is a poetic rendering of the regal-looking adult plumage of this bird, which has nocturnal habits. HERON FAMILY.

violacea: Latin for "violet-colored" refers to the back and underparts of the adult, which are shades of gray but may appear purplish in some light.

COMMON NAME: Yellow-crowned Night-Heron for the yellowish-white crown and nocturnal activity, although this species is often active during the day

OTHER NAMES: fish crane, crab-catcher, quawk

NYCTICORAX: From Greek *nyx, nyktos* (genitive) = night + Latin *corax* (Greek *korax*) = raven. "Night raven" is an allusion to the black crown and back and to the croaking call. HERON FAMILY.

nycticorax: A tautonym.

COMMON NAME: Black-crowned Night-Heron for the dark crown and nocturnal habits, although this species is frequently active during the day

OTHER NAMES: red-eye, marsh hen, squawk

ONYCHOPRION: From Greek *onyx, onychos* (genitive) = talon, claw, nail + *priōn* = a saw, jagged row, sawyer. "Serrated toe" describes the narrow, parallel, comblike projections on the long middle toe, an anatomical detail that may escape the notice of the observer. TERN FAMILY.

fuscatus: From Latin *fuscāre* = to darken. "Darkened" is an appropriate adjective for the sooty-black plumage.

COMMON NAME: Sooty Tern

OTHER NAMES: noddy, egg bird, wide-awake (for call)

OPORORNIS: From Greek *opōra* = end of summer, autumn + *ornis* = bird. "Autumn bird" expresses the perception that this genus is more frequently seen in autumn than in spring. WARBLER FAMILY.

agilis: The Latin word for "active, nimble" describes well the quick and easy movements of this species on the ground and along low branches.

COMMON NAME: Connecticut Warbler for the location of the type specimen

OTHER NAMES: bog black-throat, tamarack warbler, swamp warbler

OREOSCOPTES: From Greek *oros*, *oreos* (genitive) = mountain, hill + *skōptein* = to mock, jeer. "Mountain mocker" is a misnomer, since this monotype prefers a dry plains habitat and does not mimic the sounds of other birds. THRASHER FAMILY.

montanus: Latin for "of the mountain." The type specimen may have been taken near the mountains in western Wyoming, but this bird, which resembles a small, young mockingbird, prefers sagebrush plains and arid scrublands.

COMMON NAME: Sage Thrasher for the habitat

OTHER NAMES: mountain mockingbird, sage thrush, sage mockingbird

OREOTHLYPIS: From Greek *oros*, *oreos* (genitive) = mountain, hill + *thlypis* = a small, finchlike, seed-eating bird. This word is a variant reading of Aristotle's *thraupis*, a misnomer in either case for a warbler genus that is mostly insectivorous. "Hill bird" may describe the topography where the type specimens of birds in this resurrected genus were obtained: *O. celata* near the Loess Hills bordering the Missouri River; *O. peregrina* and *O. ruficapilla* along the western slopes of the Appalachian Range. WARBLER FAMILY.

celata: A form of Latin *celāre* = to hide, conceal. "Concealed" refers to the seldom-seen orangish patch on the crown. (Note: This is one of the few type specimens from the Upper Midwest. It was collected by Thomas Say near Omaha, Nebraska, in 1823.)

COMMON NAME: Orange-crowned Warbler

OTHER NAMES: orange-crown, dusky warbler, lutescent warbler

peregrina: Latin adjective for "foreign, strange" from *pere-grināri* = to be foreign, to wander about. "Wandering" pertains to the far-ranging migratory behavior of this species.

COMMON NAME: Tennessee Warbler for the locality of the type specimen collected on the Cumberland River in Tennessee

OTHER NAME: Tennessee swamp warbler

ruficapilla: Coined Latin adjective from *rufus* = reddish, red + *capillus* = the hair of the head. "Red-haired" alludes to the usually concealed red patch on the crown.

COMMON NAME: Nashville Warbler for the locality of the type specimen obtained near Nashville, Tennessee

OTHER NAMES: red-crowned warbler, Nashville swamp warbler, birch warbler

OXYURA: From Greek *oxys* = sharp, pointed + *oura* = tail. "Sharp-tailed" pertains to the long, pointed tail, which is often upturned, seldom fanned. DUCK FAMILY.

jamaicensis: Coined Latin adjective for "Jamaica" + Latin suffix *-ensis* = of or from a place. "Of Jamaica" designates the location of the type specimen.

COMMON NAME: Ruddy Duck for the reddish-brown color of the male's breeding plumage

OTHER NAMES: stiff-tail, bristle-tail, quill-tail, ruddy diver

PAGOPHILA: From Greek *pagos* = ice, frost + *phila* = loving, fond. "Frost friendly" is a pleasant phrase describing the preference of this genus for the far north. GULL FAMILY.

eburnea: The Latin word for "white as ivory [*ebur*]" is a description of the adult plumage.

COMMON NAME: Ivory Gull

OTHER NAMES: snow-white gull, ice bird

PANDION: Pandion was a mythical king of Athens whose daughters were changed into birds (see *Progne*); King Pandion was not so transformed. Why the French zoologist Marie Jules César Savigny (1777–1851) chose this figure from Greek myth as the name for this genus is unknown. HAWK FAMILY.

haliaetus: From Greek and Latin *haliaetos*, meaning "sea eagle, osprey" (see *Haliaeetus*).

COMMON NAME: Osprey. The etymology is Latin *os* = bone + *frangere* = to break. Pliny's *ossifraga*, meaning "osprey," also was applied to the Bearded Vulture (the Lammergeier of Eurasia), a bird reputed to carry large prey aloft to let it fall on rocks below, where it is broken apart and eaten. Another possible—but tenuous—etymology is Latin *avis* = bird + *praeda* = booty, prey, i.e., "bird of prey."

OTHER NAMES: fish hawk, fishing eagle, sea hawk

PARABUTEO: From Greek *para* = near, by, beside + *buteo*, the Latin word for "a kind of hawk or falcon, buzzard." "Kin to a buteo" implies that early taxonomists questioned this bird as a true buteo. HAWK FAMILY.

unicinctus: From Latin *uni* = one + *cinctus* = ringed, girdled. "One ring" refers to the broad white "ring" at the base of the tail.

COMMON NAME: Harris's Hawk, named for the American amateur naturalist Edward Harris (1799–1863), a friend and patron of Audubon

OTHER NAMES: bay-winged hawk, chestnut-thighed buzzard

PARKESIA: A latinized form of "Parkes's." This new genus was named for Kenneth Carroll Parkes (1922–2007), a prominent American ornithologist and taxonomist who was chief curator of the life sciences and curator of birds at the Carnegie Museum of Natural History in Pittsburgh, Pennsylvania. WARBLER FAMILY.

motacilla: From Latin *movēre* = to move + spurious Latin *cilla* = tail. "Wag-tail" is a fitting name for this tail-bobbing, teetering species.

COMMON NAME: Louisiana Waterthrush for the region of the type specimen in Louisiana Province (New France). This bird frequents waterways and has a streaked breast like that of many true thrushes.

OTHER NAMES: wag-tail warbler, water wag-tail, southern waterthrush *noveboracensis:* From Latin *novus* = new + *Eboracum*, the Roman name for the city of York in England + the suffix *-ensis* = of or from a place. "From New York" identifies where the type specimen was collected in the United States.

COMMON NAME: Northern Waterthrush for its breeding range. This bird frequents waterways and has a streaked breast like that of many true thrushes.

OTHER NAMES: water-thrush, wag-tail warbler, New York warbler

PASSER: The Latin word for "sparrow." This genus contains species once classified as weaverbirds, which are unrelated to native American sparrows. SPARROW FAMILY.

domesticus: This Latin word for "of the house" refers to the penchant for living near human dwellings and surroundings.

COMMON NAME: House Sparrow

OTHER NAMES: English sparrow, European house sparrow, hoodlum, tramp

montanus: The Latin word for "of a mountain" is apparently a misnomer. This species is not associated with mountains but, like *P. domesticus*, may live near human habitation.

COMMON NAME: Eurasian Tree Sparrow, a species introduced from Eurasia that frequently nests in trees

OTHER NAME: European tree sparrow

PASSERCULUS: From Latin *passer* = sparrow + diminutive suffix *-culus*. "Little sparrow" refers to the size. SPARROW FAMILY.

sandwichensis: A coined Latin adjective for "Sandwich" + suffix *-ensis* = of or from a place. "Of Sandwich" refers to

Sandwich Bay, Unalaska, Alaska, where the type specimen was collected.

COMMON NAME: Savannah Sparrow for the open grassland habitats

OTHER NAMES: meadow bird, ground sparrow, savannah bunting

PASSERELLA: From Latin *passer* = sparrow + diminutive suffix *-ella.* "Little sparrow" refers to the size. SPARROW FAMILY.

iliaca: The postclassical Latin word for "of or pertaining to the flanks" is a reference to the heavily marked underparts.

COMMON NAME: Fox Sparrow for the overall reddish-brown color, like that of a fox

OTHER NAMES: foxy finch, red singer, ferruginous finch

PASSERINA: From Latin *passer* = sparrow + suffix *-ina* = like, having the quality of. "Sparrowlike" points out the similarity to a sparrow in size and shape. FINCH FAMILY.

amoena: The Latin word for "charming, delightful" is a fitting description of this attractive bird.

COMMON NAME: Lazuli Bunting from postclassical Latin *lazulum*, a semiprecious stone that is azure blue, which describes the rich blue head, back, and wings of the adult male

OTHER NAME: lazuli painted finch

caerulea: This Latin word for "blue, azure" highlights the bright blue plumage of the adult male.

COMMON NAME: Blue Grosbeak

OTHER NAMES: big indigo, blue pop

ciris: The name for a kind of bird in Greek myth:

> On King Nisus' head
> Among the honored grayness, there was growing
> One shining purple lock: this he must keep
> Or lose his mighty kingdom, so the legend has it.
> —Ovid, *Metamorphoses*, Book VIII
>   (translated by Rolfe Humphries)

Scylla, daughter of King Nisus, whose city was being besieged by King Minos of Crete, fell in love with her father's enemy. To win the favor of Minos, Scylla cut the fatal purple lock from her father's head while he was sleeping and presented it to Minos. Appalled by this immoral act, Minos spurned both the gift and the giver and sailed for Crete. Scylla, clinging to his departing ship, was attacked by her vengeful father—now an osprey—causing her to release her hold. While she was falling into the sea, the gods changed her into a bird called the *ciris*.

Ciris is *Keiris* in Greek from *keirein* = to clip, cut short. The name, then, means "the shearer," which is appropriate for Scylla's action. Linnaeus, in naming this species, did not use *ciris* as "the shearer" but as the purple lock shorn from the head of King Nisus. The reference is to the color of the head of this species.

COMMON NAME: Painted Bunting for the full palette of brilliant plumage colors—blue, red, green, yellow—of the adult male

OTHER NAMES: painted finch, nonpareil, paradise finch

cyanea: A Latin word for "dark blue" (Greek *kyaneos*) that refers to the deep indigo-blue color of the adult male.

COMMON NAME: Indigo Bunting

OTHER NAMES: blue canary, indigo finch, indigo bird

PELECANUS: The Latin word for "pelican" (Greek *pelekan*). PELICAN FAMILY.

erythrorhynchos: From Greek *erythros* = red + *rhynchos* = bill, beak. "Red beak" is somewhat misleading, since the bill and its voluminous pouch are not red but orange or salmon-colored.

COMMON NAME: American White Pelican for its range and the plumage of this very large white bird

OTHER NAMES: rough-billed pelican, common pelican

occidentalis: The Latin word for "western, westerly" locates this species' range in the Western Hemisphere.

COMMON NAME: Brown Pelican for the rich black back of the crown and nape of the breeding adult, which has an overall brownish appearance

OTHER NAMES: alcatraz, common pelican

PERDIX: The Greek and Latin word for "partridge." The name appears in several Greek myths: e.g., Perdix was the clever nephew of Daedalus, who, out of jealousy, threw him from the Acropolis to his death. While falling, Perdix was transformed by Athene into a partridge (Ovid). QUAIL FAMILY.

perdix: A bird that remembers its long fall and keeps close to the ground. A tautonym.

COMMON NAME: Gray Partridge for the general color of plumage

OTHER NAMES: Hungarian partridge, Bohemian partridge, redtail

PERISOREUS: Probably coined from Greek *peri* = around + *sōreuein* = to heap up. "Heaper-upper" is a good name for this genus, which is renowned for stealing and storing food. JAY FAMILY.

canadensis: Coined Latin adjective for "Canada" + suffix *-ensis* = of or from a place. "Of Canada" identifies the locality of the type specimen taken in Quebec.

COMMON NAME: Gray Jay for the predominant color of the plumage

OTHER NAMES: camp robber, whiskey jack, lumberjack

PETROCHELIDON: From Greek *petros* = rock, stone + *chelidōn* = a swallow. "Rock swallow" refers to the original nesting sites on cliffs—and now on bridges and buildings. SWALLOW FAMILY.

fulva: A Latin word for "tawny, reddish-brown" that describes the color of the forehead and rump and the buffy throat and nape.

COMMON NAME: Cave Swallow for the nest sites in caves, culverts, and overhanging cliffs

OTHER NAME: buff-throated swallow

pyrrhonota: From Greek *pyrros* = flame-colored, reddish + *nōton* = the back. "Red-backed" alludes to the reddish-orange rump (and face and throat).

COMMON NAME: Cliff Swallow

OTHER NAMES: moon-fronted swallow, crescent swallow, jug swallow (for nest shape)

PEUCAEA: From Greek dialect *peukaeis* = of the fir (*peukē*). "Those of the firs" implies the habitat and feeding areas in open, grassy coniferous woods, undergrowth, brambles, and thickets. SPARROW FAMILY.

aestivalis: The Latin word for "summerlike, pertaining to summer [*aestas*]." The application of this name is uncertain. Perhaps it refers to the season in which the breeding range expands into the Midwest and thus when these birds are more frequently seen.

COMMON NAME: Bachman's Sparrow, named for John Bachman (1790–1874), a Lutheran pastor and dedicated amateur ornithologist of Charleston, South Carolina, by his good friend John James Audubon

OTHER NAME: pine-woods sparrow

cassinii: A latinized form of "Cassin's." This species was named for John Cassin.

COMMON NAME: Cassin's Sparrow

OTHER NAMES: None found

PHALACROCORAX: Pliny's word for "cormorant" from Greek *phalakros* = bald-headed + *korax* = raven or crow (Latin *corax*). "Bald raven" applies because these birds have a hooked, ravenlike beak; the impression of baldness is given by the skin of the extensive gular pouch and the pale feathers on the face of some species, especially the Eurasian *P. carbo.* CORMORANT FAMILY.

auritus: The Latin word for "eared" refers to the small feathered crests or plumes—sometimes white—on each side of the head of prebreeding birds.

COMMON NAME: Double-crested Cormorant

OTHER NAMES: water raven, shag, crow duck

brasilianus: A coined Latin adjective for "Brasilia" + suffix *-anus* = of or from. "Of Brazil" designates the region where the type specimen was collected.

COMMON NAME: Neotropic Cormorant for its range from South and Central America into the southern United States

OTHER NAMES: olivaceous cormorant, Brazilian cormorant

PHALAENOPTILUS: From Greek *phalaina* = whale; but, curiously, this word also means "moth" + *ptilon* = feather, plumage, wing. "Moth-winged" pertains to the rounded wings and mothlike flight. NIGHTJAR FAMILY.

nuttallii: The latinized form of "Nuttall's." This bird was named for Thomas Nuttall (1786–1859), who was born and died in England, although he spent many years in the United States. Primarily a botanist whose *Genera of North American Plants* (1818) gained worldwide renown, Nuttall also became an accomplished ornithologist. A friend of William Bartram, William Brewster, John James Audubon, John Kirk Townsend, Thomas Say, and other ornithologists, Nuttall traveled extensively, discovered many new species of birds, including this one, and earned a reputation for his scientific work. He became a lecturer and botanical curator at Harvard University, where he wrote *A Manual of the Ornithology of the United States and Canada* (in two parts, 1832 and 1834). Nuttall had a long and productive career in the United States and is recognized as one of the great American ornithologists.

COMMON NAME: Common Poorwill for this most numerous of American nightjars and a name that is imitative of the call

OTHER NAMES: dusky poor-will, Nuttall's poor-will

PHALAROPUS: From Greek *phalaris* = coot + *pous* = foot. "Coot-footed" refers to the lobed, semipalmated toes, similar to those of a coot. These flapped toes make possible the unique behavior of birds in this genus to spin on the water to stir up food. PHALAROPE FAMILY.

fulicarius: From Latin *fulica* = coot, waterbird + suffix *-arius* = having the nature of. "Cootlike" alludes to the lobed toes, similar to those of a coot.

COMMON NAME: Red Phalarope, a boreal bird with reddish-brown underparts on both the male and female in breeding plumage

OTHER NAMES: sea snipe, brown bank-bird, gray phalarope, whale-bird

lobatus: A coined Latin adjective from Greek *lobos* = lobe. "Lobed" refers to the rounded flaps on the toes.

COMMON NAME: Red-necked Phalarope for the reddish-brown neck and collar of the female breeding plumage on this boreal bird

OTHER NAMES: northern phalarope, web-footed peep, bank-bird

tricolor: Postclassical Latin word for "of three colors," which refers to the cinnamon-tinged throat, whitish underparts, and black streak through the eye to the nape.

COMMON NAME: Wilson's Phalarope, a small, graceful swimmer named for Alexander Wilson

OTHER NAME: summer phalarope

PHASIANUS: The Greek *phasianos* is the word for "pheasant." Literally "the Phasian bird," the pheasant was abundant where the river Phasis flows into the Black Sea. PHEASANT FAMILY.

colchicus: From Latin *Colchis* (Greek *Kolchis*), an ancient country through which the river Phasis flows. Colchis was the home of Medea, the Golden Fleece, and the destination of the Argonauts. "Colchian" identifies the place where large numbers of pheasants were reported in ancient times to be feeding near the mouth of the river.

COMMON NAME: Ring-necked Pheasant for the white collar on the neck of the male

OTHER NAMES: ring-neck, Chinese pheasant, cackle-bird

PHEUCTICUS: From Greek *pheuktikos* = inclined to avoid (from *pheugein* = to flee, avoid). "Bashful" expresses the perceived shy nature of birds in this genus. GROSBEAK FAMILY.

ludovicianus: A postclassical Latin adjective for *Ludovicus* (Louis XIV), meaning "of Louisiana (Territory)," indicates the region of the type specimen.

COMMON NAME: Rose-breasted Grosbeak for the rose-red bib on the breast of the adult male

OTHER NAMES: rose-breast, summer grosbeak, throat-cut

melanocephalus: From Greek *melas*, *melanos* (genitive) = black, dark + *kephalē* = the head. "Black head" describes the head of the adult male.

COMMON NAME: Black-headed Grosbeak

OTHER NAMES: blackhead, western grosbeak

PHILOMACHUS: From Greek *philos* = fond, loving + *machē* = battle, fight, combat. "Fond of fighting" describes well the male's aggressive behavior on courtship leks. SANDPIPER FAMILY.

pugnax: The Latin word for "combative, warlike" is appropriate for the pugnacity of this species during courtship. This bird may be overnamed.

COMMON NAME: Ruff for the extraordinary ruffle of long feathers around the neck of the male, which are erected in a showy display during courtship. The female is called a "reeve," the origin of which is unknown.

OTHER NAME: combatiente

PICA: Latin word for "magpie." CROW FAMILY.

hudsonia: Coined Latin adjective for "Hudson" + suffix -ia = pertaining to. "Hudsonian" does not refer to Hudson Bay, which is east of this bird's range. The reference instead is to the Hudson Bay drainage basin (also known as the Hudson Bay Territories or Prince Rupert's Land). The type specimen was collected in 1819 at the Hudson Bay Company's Cumberland House, Saskatchewan, Canada, 400 to 500 miles inland and well within the range of this species.

COMMON NAME: Black-billed Magpie for the beak color

OTHER NAME: American magpie

PICOIDES: From Latin picus = woodpecker + Greek suffix -oides = similar to, resembling. "Woodpecker-like" alludes to the general appearance and behavior of birds in this genus. WOODPECKER FAMILY.

arcticus: From Greek arktikos = near the Great Bear (arktos, i.e., Ursa Major), northern, arctic. "Northern" defines the general range in the United States.

COMMON NAME: Black-backed Woodpecker for the solidly black back

OTHER NAMES: little black woodpecker, arctic three-toed woodpecker

dorsalis: A form of Latin dorsualis, meaning "of or pertaining to the back [dorsum]," refers to the mostly black back marked with a distinctive but variable white barring pattern.

COMMON NAME: American Three-toed Woodpecker for the two toes pointing forward and one backward (Most woodpeckers have two toes pointed forward and two backward.)

OTHER NAMES: white-backed three-toed woodpecker, alpine woodpecker

pubescens: From Latin *pubescere* = to put on the down of puberty. "Becoming downy" alludes to the dainty, fluffy tuft of modified feathers (nasal bristles) at the base of the bill, which filter debris, the result of drilling into bark and wood. This bird is thought to look smaller and younger than *P. villosus.*

COMMON NAME: Downy Woodpecker

OTHER NAMES: little woodpecker, spotted woodpecker, black and white

scalaris: The Latin word for "of or belonging to a flight of steps [*scalae*] or a ladder" is an appropriate allusion to the alternating black-and-white plumage on the back, which resembles the pattern of rungs on a ladder.

COMMON NAME: Ladder-backed Woodpecker

OTHER NAMES: cactus woodpecker, speckle-cheek

villosus: The Latin word for "hairy, shaggy, rough" describes the stiffer, but less conspicuous, nasal bristles than those of *P. pubescens.* In addition, *villosus* is larger and thought to look more mature than *pubescens.*

COMMON NAME: Hairy Woodpecker

OTHER NAMES: big woodpecker, white-breasted woodpecker

PINICOLA: From Latin *pinus* = pine tree + *colere* = to reside, inhabit. "Pine dweller" pertains to the favored habitat in conifers, especially in summer. GROSBEAK FAMILY.

enucleator: From Latin *enucleāre* = to take out the kernels + suffix *-tor* = agent, one that does. "Nut picker" affirms the method of obtaining pine seeds, a preferred diet.

COMMON NAME: Pine Grosbeak

OTHER NAMES: Canadian grosbeak, pine bullfinch, mope (it often sits motionless)

PIPILO: Latin first-person singular of *pipilāre* = to chirp, peep. "Chirp" is onomatopoetic, as is the common name, towhee. TOWHEE FAMILY.

chlorurus: From Greek *chloros* = green + *oura* = tail. "Green tail" describes the olive-green tail (and wings).

COMMON NAME: Green-tailed Towhee

OTHER NAMES: chestnut-crowned towhee, green-tailed bunting

erythrophthalmus: From Greek *erythros* = red + *ophthalmos* = eye. "Red eye" emphasizes the eye color of the more northern group.

COMMON NAME: Eastern Towhee for its range in the United States

OTHER NAMES: rufous-sided towhee, brush robin, red-eyed towhee, chewink (for call)

maculatus: A Latin word for "spotted" (*maculāre* = to spot, stain), which refers to the irregular white spotting on the scapulars and wings.

COMMON NAME: Spotted Towhee

OTHER NAME: Oregon towhee

PIRANGA: Apparently a form of *tijepiranga*, a native Tupi (Brazil) word for "a small bird." In the nine-volume *Histoire Naturelle des Oiseaux* (1770–1783) by Georges-Louis Leclerc, Count de Buffon (1707–1788), the *tijepiranga* is described as a lark-sized bird with a red body, neck, and head and black wings and tail. TANAGER FAMILY.

ludoviciana: A postclassical Latin adjective for *Ludovicus* (Louis XIV), meaning "of Louisiana (Territory)," pertains to the region where the type specimen was taken on the Lewis and Clark Expedition in what is now Idaho.

COMMON NAME: Western Tanager for its range in the United States

OTHER NAME: Louisiana tanager

olivacea: Postclassical Latin word for "olive-green," which describes the plumage color of the female and of the adult male in winter.

COMMON NAME: Scarlet Tanager for the vivid red summer plumage of the adult male

OTHER NAMES: black-winged redbird, firebird

rubra: This Latin word for "red, ruddy" refers to the rose-red plumage of the adult male.

COMMON NAME: Summer Tanager for the more northern presence of this species in summer

OTHER NAMES: summer redbird, rose tanager, calico warbler, bee bird

PLATALEA: This word and *platea* are synonymous Latin words (Greek *plateia* = flat, wide, broad) for "the spoonbill," a clear reference to the spatulate bill. IBIS FAMILY.

ajaja: A Tupi (Brazil) word for Roseate Spoonbill. This word and many other Tupi words for flora and fauna are found in the eight-volume *Historia Naturalis Brasiliae* (1648) by Georg Markgraf (1610–1644), a German botanist and astronomer, and Willem Piso (1611–1678), a Dutch physician and naturalist. Both men served Dutch colonial and other interests in Brazil, which they explored for zoological and botanical specimens.

COMMON NAME: Roseate Spoonbill for the pink to red plumage and the spatulate bill

OTHER NAMES: rosy spoonbill, pink curlew

PLECTROPHENAX: From Greek *plēktron* (Latin *plectrum*) = a little stick used to strike the strings of a lyre, and, oddly enough, a cock's spur + *phenax* = a cheat, imposter. The original name of this genus was *Plectrophanes* from Greek *plēktron* + *phanein* = to appear, display, thus meaning "displaying a spur," for the long hind claw. Leonhard Hess Stejneger changed the name to *Plectrophenax*, meaning "fake spur," to indicate, perhaps, that this genus differs in this anatomical feature from *Calcarius*, the longspur genus. Stejneger (1851–1943), a native of Norway, became assistant curator of birds and then head curator of biology at the Smithsonian Institution. He did much work in Alaska and the Bering Sea region. SPARROW FAMILY.

nivalis: The Latin word for "snowy, wintry" alludes to both the boreal range of this species and the predominantly white plumage of both sexes.

COMMON NAME: Snow Bunting

OTHER NAMES: snow lark, snowbird, snowflake

PLEGADIS: From Greek *plēgas, plēgados* (genitive) = sickle, scythe, scimitar. "Sickle" is a description of the curved bill. IBIS FAMILY.

chihi: The Quechuan word for "pasture, grassy area." This name was given in 1817 by Louis Vieillot (1748–1831), a French ornithologist. The type specimen was taken in Paraguay, where Quechuan—or a dialect thereof—was spoken. It is possible that this species was often seen feeding in wet, grassy meadows (*chihi*), and this word may have been the Quechuan name for this bird. See *Gavia immer* for a similar situation. Some sources suggest that *chihi* is an echoic name for the bird.

COMMON NAME: White-faced Ibis for the narrow border of white feathers that surrounds the reddish face in breeding plumage

OTHER NAMES: white-faced glossy ibis, black curlew

falcinellus: From Latin *falx, falcis* (genitive) = sickle, scythe, pruning hook + diminutive suffix *-ellus*. "Little sickle" refers to the curved bill.

COMMON NAME: Glossy Ibis for its shiny breeding plumage

OTHER NAMES: green ibis, bay ibis, black curlew

PLUVIALIS: The Latin word for "of or pertaining to rain [*pluvia*]." The name plover has its origin in *pluvia*, and plovers have been associated with rain in myth and legend since early times. Some suggestions for this association are that the bird sings in the rain (the German word for plover is *Regenpfeifer* = rain piper); the plumage of some plovers is spotted with "raindrops"; the bird is easy to catch in the rain; and it migrates to escape the rainy season. PLOVER FAMILY.

dominica: A latinized adjective meaning "from Santo Domingo (Hispaniola)," the island location of the type specimen.

COMMON NAME: American Golden-Plover for the breeding range in North America and for the adult plumage color in summer

OTHER NAMES: lesser golden plover, spotted plover, brass-back, black-breast

squatarola: According to Coues and others, this is an Italian dialect word for, perhaps, the Grey Plover, the common name in Europe for this species.

COMMON NAME: Black-bellied Plover for the distinctive dark face, throat, and belly

OTHER NAMES: silverback, whistling plover, mud plover, black-breast

PODICEPS: This is another word with an aberrant etymology. It seems to be a misprint or misspelling of the original *Podicipes* from the Latin *podex, podicis* (genitive) = rump + *pes* = foot. The term "rump-footed" is an allusion to the position of the legs set far back on the body and appearing to extend from the rump. Whatever the previous etymological wanderings, the name for this genus appears as *Podiceps* several times in the 10-volume *A General History of Birds* (1821–1828) by John Latham (1790–1837), who was a leading English ornithologist of his time. The truncated name *Podiceps* has been retained for a genus and a species. GREBE FAMILY.

auritus: The Latin word for "eared" refers to the prominent feathered tufts on the head, giving the impression of slightly protuberant "horns." "Eared" but *not* the Eared Grebe, as one would infer from the Latin name.

COMMON NAME: Horned Grebe

OTHER NAMES: pipe-neck, dusty grebe, water-witch

grisegena: Postclassical Latin *griseus* = gray + Latin *gena* (Greek *genys*) = cheek. "Gray-cheeked" refers to the conspicuous color of the cheeks and throat in all plumages.

COMMON NAME: Red-necked Grebe for the rufous neck in breeding plumage

OTHER NAMES: laughing diver, Holboell's diver

nigricollis: Latin *niger* = black, dark + postclassical Latin *collis* (from *collum*) = neck. "Dark-necked" describes not only the neck but also the head and back in breeding plumage.

COMMON NAME: Eared Grebe for the buff-colored cockades on the sides of the head

OTHER NAMES: black-necked grebe, eared diver

PODILYMBUS: A word tortuously coined from the previous aberrant genus name *Podiceps*, meaning "grebe," and the Greek *kolymbos* = a diving bird, a grebe (Aristotle and other writers of antiquity). Linnaeus used the Greek word for his grebe genus *Colymbus*. Thus, *Podilymbus*, a name of fractured components, means "a rump-footed diving bird" or, as some have suggested, a "grebe grebe." At least one gets the idea! GREBE FAMILY.

podiceps: See genus *Podiceps*.

COMMON NAME: Pied-billed Grebe for the black band on the whitish bill

OTHER NAMES: dabchick, thick-billed grebe, hell-diver

POECILE: From Greek *poikilos* = many-colored, pied, of varied colors. "Polychromatic" expresses the variety of colors on birds of this genus and the several colors on each species. CHICKADEE FAMILY.

atricapillus: The Latin word for "black-haired" (from *ater* = black + *capillus* = the hair of the head) describes the black "cap" of head feathers.

COMMON NAME: Black-capped Chickadee

OTHER NAMES: common chickadee, black-capped titmouse, long-tailed chickadee

carolinensis: Coined Latin adjective for "Carolina" + suffix *-ensis* = of or from a place. "Of Carolina" refers to the locality of the type specimen collected near Charleston, South Carolina.

COMMON NAME: Carolina Chickadee

OTHER NAMES: southern chickadee, plumbeous chickadee

gambeli: A latinized form of "Gambel's." This bird was named for William Gambel (1823–1849), a naturalist and bird collector, who was a protégé of Thomas Nuttall (see *Phalaenoptilus* *nuttallii*). Gambel, a daring traveler, was a pioneer ornithologist in the Southwest.

COMMON NAME: Mountain Chickadee for the breeding range, up to 10,000 feet, along the Rocky Mountains

OTHER NAME: short-tailed chickadee

hudsonicus: Coined Latin adjective for "Hudson" (Bay) + suffix *-icus* = of or pertaining to. "Of Hudson Bay" identifies the locality in Canada where the type specimen was taken.

COMMON NAME: Boreal Chickadee for the very northern range in North America

OTHER NAMES: brown-capped chickadee, brownie, Hudsonian chickadee

POLIOPTILA: From Greek *polios* = gray, hoary + *ptilon* = feather, plumage. "Gray-feathered" is a description of the bluish-gray upperparts of both the male and female. WARBLER FAMILY.

caerulea: The Latin word for "blue" emphasizes the plumage color.

COMMON NAME: Blue-gray Gnatcatcher, which combines both the generic and specific descriptions

OTHER NAMES: common gnatcatcher, little blue-gray wren, blue-gray flycatcher

POOECETES: From Greek *poē* = grass + *oiketēs* = inhabitant, dweller. "Grass dweller" refers to the habitat. SPARROW FAMILY.

gramineus: The Latin word for "covered with grass, grassy" is another reference to the habitat.

COMMON NAME: Vesper Sparrow, which often sings in the evening (*vesper* in Latin)

OTHER NAMES: bay-winged bunting, grass sparrow, pasture-bird

PORPHYRIO: The Latin word for "a species of waterfowl" and Greek *porphyrion* for a "red-colored waterbird." Both words are derived from the Greek *porphyreos* = purple. "Purple waterbird" describes the plumage color and the marshy habitat. RAIL FAMILY.

martinicus: A latinized form of "Martinique" (West Indies) refers to the island on which the type specimen was obtained.

COMMON NAME: Purple Gallinule for the color of the head, neck, and breast

OTHER NAMES: blue peter, marsh hen

PORZANA: Most sources believe that this is a form of the Italian dialect word *sporzana*, a name for smaller rails. RAIL FAMILY.

carolina: A Latin adjective form for "of or from Carolina," in this case, the colonial region of the southeastern United States, where this bird is common during migration.

COMMON NAME: Sora, believed to be an American Indian name for this bird

OTHER NAMES: sora rail, common rail, chicken-bill

PROGNE: A form of the Greek *Proknē* and the Latin *Procnē*. Procne was the daughter of King Pandion of Athens, wife of Tereus, and sister of Philomela. In a gory Greek myth, Procne is changed into a swallow, and Philomela into a nightingale. These transformations are reversed in some versions of the myth. SWALLOW FAMILY.

subis: This is "a kind of bird that breaks eagles' eggs" (Pliny). Why this name is used for this species is a mystery.

COMMON NAME: Purple Martin for the purplish-black, glossy plumage

OTHER NAMES: black martin, purple swallow, gourd martin, house martin

PROTONOTARIA: From Greek *prōtos* = first, foremost + Latin *notarius* = scribe, secretary. "First secretary" refers to high officials in the Vatican, who once wore yellow robes; the allusion is to the similarly colored plumage of this genus. WARBLER FAMILY.

citrea: From Latin *citrus* = the citron (lemon) tree. "Lemon" emphasizes the striking yellow plumage.

COMMON NAME: Prothonotary Warbler

OTHER NAMES: golden swamp warbler, willow warbler

PYROCEPHALUS: From Greek *pyr, pyros* (genitive) = fire + *kephalē* = the head. "Head of fire" refers to the bright red, flame-colored head of the adult male. FLYCATCHER FAMILY.

rubinus: The postclassical Latin word for "ruby-red" describes well the bright red head and underparts of the adult male.

COMMON NAME: Vermilion Flycatcher for the third and last description of the brilliant red plumage

OTHER NAMES: None found

QUISCALUS:

Many etymologies have been
proposed for both the generic name
and the similar specific *quiscula*. Most recent sources, however, agree that both words are forms of the postclassical Latin
quiscalis = quail. It is not likely that Linnaeus, who named this
genus, confused the taxonomies of the quail and grackle. We
suggest that he was marking the similarities of the calls of grackles and those of many quail species, both noted for their loud,
percussive, strident sounds.

The name for "quail" in many languages is onomatopoetic:
coacula (Vulgar Latin); *quahtala* (Old High German); *quaccula*
(Medieval Latin); *quaglia* (Italian); *kwakkel* (Dutch). Or the
name could have been a Native American word for a quail-like
bird that made such sounds, e.g., the Inuit word *aqissiaq* for the
Rock Ptarmigan (*Lagopus muta*), a croaking bird of the tundra,
could qualify here. All these onomatopoetic names contain one
or more voiceless stops: *c*, *ck*, *k*, *q*, sounds heard in the calls of
many quail and quail-like birds and grackles. The *chack*, *chuck*,
kek-kek-kek, *kerr*, *ki-ki-ki-ki*, for example, are some sounds emit-
ted by birds in these genera. We propose, therefore, that the
words *Quiscalus* and *quiscula* are onomatopoetic names assigned
by Linnaeus to this genus and species. BLACKBIRD FAMILY.

mexicanus: Coined Latin adjective for "Mexico" + suffix
-anus = of or from. "Of Mexico" applies to the locality of the
type specimen taken in Vera Cruz.

COMMON NAME: Great-tailed Grackle for the remarkably
long tail

OTHER NAMES: jackdaw, crow blackbird

quiscula: Almost an anagram of the generic name.

COMMON NAME: Common Grackle for the widest-ranging
North American grackle

OTHER NAMES: keel-tailed grackle, bronzed grackle, purple
grackle

RALLUS: Postclassical Latin word for "a rail." RAIL FAMILY.

elegans: The Latin word for "elegant" refers to the handsome appearance of this species.

COMMON NAME: King Rail for its large size

OTHER NAMES: great red-breasted rail, freshwater marsh hen

limicola: From Latin *limus* = mud, slime + *colere* = to live in a place, inhabit. "Mud dweller" refers to a habitat of freshwater and brackish marshes.

COMMON NAME: Virginia Rail. The type specimen was collected in Pennsylvania, then considered part of the Colonial Virginia region.

OTHER NAMES: little red-breasted rail, long-billed rail

RECURVIROSTRA: From Latin *recurvus* = curving backward, bending + *rostrum* = beak. "Recurved bill" describes the upturned beak. STILT FAMILY.

americana: A latinized adjective form for "of or from America," which identifies the breeding range in North America.

COMMON NAME: American Avocet for the breeding range of this showy, graceful wading bird

OTHER NAMES: blue-stocking, blue-shanks, yellow-necked snipe

REGULUS: The Latin word for "a little king, prince" alludes to the small size, colorful "crown," and commanding behavior of birds in this genus. WARBLER FAMILY.

calendula: A coined Latin word for "glowing" (from *calēre* = to glow with heat) that describes the red patch on the crown of the male.

COMMON NAME: Ruby-crowned Kinglet for the infrequently seen red crown of the male

OTHER NAMES: ruby crown, ruby-crowned wren, ruby-crowned warbler

satrapa: The Latin word (Greek *satrapēs*) for "a viceroy, provincial governor," who might be inclined to wear a crown.

COMMON NAME: Golden-crowned Kinglet for the orange patch on the crown of the male, yellow on the female

OTHER NAMES: gold-crest, flame-crest, fiery-crowned wren

RHODOSTETHIA: From Greek *rhodon* = a rose + *stēthos* = breast. "Rose-breasted" describes the pinkish coloration of the head and body of the summer adult. GULL FAMILY.

rosea: The Latin word for "rose-colored."

COMMON NAME: Ross's Gull, named for Sir James Clark Ross (1800–1862), a British Royal Navy officer, polar explorer, and discoverer of the northern magnetic pole, who collected this type specimen on the Melville Peninsula in the Canadian Arctic in 1823

OTHER NAMES: rosy gull, wedge-tailed gull

RHYNCHOPHANES: From Greek *rhynchos* = bill, beak + *phanēs* (a form of the verb *phainein* = to display, exhibit, be visible) = something seen, conspicuous. "Prominent bill" affirms the longest, heaviest bill of all longspur species. SPARROW FAMILY.

mccownii: A latinized form of "McCown's." This bird is named for John Porter McCown (1815–1879), who, as a US Army officer stationed in Texas, obtained the type specimen between San Antonio and the Rio Grande in 1851.

COMMON NAME: McCown's Longspur

OTHER NAMES: McCown's bunting, ground lark, rufous-winged lark bunting

RIPARIA: A postclassical Latin word meaning "that which frequents the bank [*ripa*] of a river." This is an appropriate name for the birds of this genus, which nest in sand and gravel embankments along waterways. SWALLOW FAMILY.

riparia: A tautonym.

COMMON NAME: Bank Swallow

OTHER NAMES: sand swallow, bank martin

RISSA: A latinized form of the Icelandic words *ritsa* and *rita*, meaning "kittiwake." GULL FAMILY.

tridactyla: From the Greek prefix *tri-* = three + *daktylos* = digit, toe, finger. "Three-toed" calls attention to the three toes, which appear large in contrast to the vestigial hind toe (hallux).

COMMON NAME: Black-legged Kittiwake for the color of the legs and the onomatopoetic call

OTHER NAMES: Atlantic kittiwake, frost gull, pick-me-up (for call)

SALPINCTES: A latinized form of Greek *salpinktēs*, meaning "trumpeter" (from *salpinx* = trumpet), which expresses the loud, varying songs of this genus. WREN FAMILY.

obsoletus: The Latin word for "worn out, shabbily dressed" alludes to the drab brown plumage.

COMMON NAME: Rock Wren for the habitat among rocky crevices and ledges

OTHER NAME: common rock wren

SAYORNIS: Eponymous name for Thomas Say (1787–1834) + Greek *ornis* = bird. "Say's bird" honors Thomas Say, "the father of North American entomology" and an important contributor to the developing sciences of both conchology and ornithology. A founding member of the Academy of Natural History in Philadelphia, Say collected a number of type specimens while a member of Stephen H. Long's expedition to the Rocky Mountains (1819–1820). FLYCATCHER FAMILY.

phoebe: The meaning of this name remains clouded. It may be onomatopoetic; it may be an alternative of pewee, a common name for flycatchers; or it may refer to Phoebe, another name for Diana, who, in Greek myth, was the moon goddess. The name Phoebe comes from the Greek *phoibos* = pure, bright, shining, radiant. Birder's choice!

COMMON NAME: Eastern Phoebe for its general range in the United States

OTHER NAMES: bridge phoebe, water pewee, wagtail

saya: A latinized adjective form of "Say's" results in the name *Sayornis saya*, meaning "Say's Say's bird." This bird may be overnamed.

COMMON NAME: Say's Phoebe

OTHER NAMES: Say's pewee, flycatcher

SCOLOPAX: From the Latin *scolopax* and Greek *skolopax* = woodcock. SNIPE FAMILY.

minor: The Latin word for "smaller, lesser" indicates that this species is somewhat smaller than its Eurasian counterpart (*S. rusticola*).

COMMON NAME: American Woodcock for its range in the eastern United States and its open woodland habitat

OTHER NAMES: timber-doodle, bog-bird, big-eyes, wood snipe, whistler

SEIURUS: From Greek *seiein* = to shake, brandish + *oura* = tail. "Tail bobber" describes the habitual action of raising and lowering the tail. WARBLER FAMILY.

aurocapilla: Latin *aurum* = gold + *capillus* = the hair of the head (*caput*). "Golden-haired" highlights the color of the crown feathers.

COMMON NAME: Ovenbird for the dome-shaped nest built on or very near the ground

OTHER NAMES: teacher-bird (for call), golden-crowned thrush, accentor

SELASPHORUS: From Greek *selas* = a flash, blaze, lightning + *phoreus* = carrier, bearer (from *phorein* = to bear, carry). "Flash bearer" reflects the dazzling reddish blaze of the male's gorget. HUMMINGBIRD FAMILY.

calliope: Calliope, one of nine Greek Muses, is the Muse of epic poetry. All the Muses were beautiful, lovable, and inspirational—like this species.

COMMON NAME: Calliope Hummingbird

OTHER NAMES: None found

platycercus: From Greek *platys* = broad, wide + *kerkos* = tail. "Broad tail" describes the long, wide tail when fanned.

COMMON NAME: Broad-tailed Hummingbird

OTHER NAME: broad-tailed hummer

rufus: The Latin word for "red, reddish" emphasizes the reddish-orange plumage and gorget of the male.

COMMON NAME: Rufous Hummingbird

OTHER NAME: rufous hummer

SETOPHAGA: Greek *sēs, sētos* (genitive) = moth + *phagein* = to eat. "Moth eater" is a general term for birds whose diet consists mostly of insects. WARBLER FAMILY.

americana: A latinized adjective form of "America," which describes this bird's range in the eastern United States and Canada.

COMMON NAME: Northern Parula distinguishes this species from that of the Tropical Parula (*S. pitiayumi*), which ranges from Mexico to South Texas. The name Parula is derived from the Latin *parus*, meaning "titmouse," and the diminutive suffix *-ula*, meaning "little," which may be translated as "a little bird."

OTHER NAME: blue yellowback

caerulescens: A form of the inferred Latin verb *caerulescere* = to become blue, i.e., slightly blue. "Bluish" describes the plumage of the male.

COMMON NAME: Black-throated Blue Warbler for the male's black throat, cheeks, and sides and for the blue upperparts

OTHER NAMES: black-throat, blue flycatcher

castanea: The Latin word for "chestnut tree, chestnut" alludes to the coloring on the head, breast, and sides of the male.

COMMON NAME: Bay-breasted Warbler for the reddish-brown breast of the male

OTHER NAMES: autumn warbler, bay-breast, little chocolate-breast

cerulea: The Latin word for "blue, blue-green" describes the blue upperparts of the male and the greenish mantle and crown of the female.

COMMON NAME: Cerulean Warbler

OTHER NAMES: blue warbler, azure warbler

citrina: From the Greek word *kitrinos*, meaning "of citron," which describes the distinct "lemon-colored" face and breast.

COMMON NAME: Hooded Warbler for the black cowl on the head of the male

OTHER NAMES: black-headed warbler, hooded flycatching warbler, mitered warbler

coronata: A form of the Latin *coronāre* = to crown, wreath. "Crowned" refers to the patch of yellow on the crown of the male.

COMMON NAME: Yellow-rumped Warbler for the coloration on both male and female

OTHER NAMES: myrtle warbler, golden-crowned flycatcher (eastern group); Audubon's warbler, black-fronted warbler (western group); butter-butt, yellow-rump

discolor: The Latin word for "particolored, variegated, of another color." "Of varied colors" is a general description of the yellow underparts, black streaking on the neck, and chestnut streaks on the back.

COMMON NAME: Prairie Warbler for a habitat (in which this species is rarely found)

OTHER NAMES: None found

dominica: A latinized form of "Santo Domingo (Hispaniola)" identifies the island where the type specimen was collected.

COMMON NAME: Yellow-throated Warbler for the dazzling throat feathers of both the male and female

OTHER NAMES: sycamore warbler, yellow-throated creeper

fusca: The Latin word for "dark, dusky" refers to the black crown and back.

COMMON NAME: Blackburnian Warbler. It is unclear for whom this warbler was named. Both Anna Blackburne (1726–1793) and her brother, Ashton (ca. 1730–ca. 1780), were avid amateur British ornithologists and bird collectors. At one time (1788), the binomial for this species was *Motacilla blackburniae*, the *-ae* female suffix implying that the name was meant to commemorate Anna. Others suggest, however, that the bird was named to honor Ashton—or Anna—or both.

OTHER NAMES: orange-throated warbler, fire-brand, torch-bird

kirtlandii: A latinized form of "Kirtland's." This bird is named for Jared Potter Kirtland (1793–1877), a physician, ornithologist, and Ohio state legislator who helped found the Cleveland

Medical College and the Cleveland Academy of Natural Sciences, later to become the Cleveland Museum of Natural History. (Note: The type specimen, one of the few taken from the Upper Midwest, was collected near Cleveland, Ohio.)

COMMON NAME: Kirtland's Warbler

OTHER NAME: jack-pine bird

magnolia: This coined Latin adjective probably refers to the magnolia trees from which the type specimen was taken by Alexander Wilson.

COMMON NAME: Magnolia Warbler

OTHER NAMES: black and yellow warbler, spotted warbler

nigrescens: A form of the Latin verb *nigrescere* = to become black, i.e., slightly black. "Blackish" is an inadequate adjective for the strongly variegated black, white, and gray plumage.

COMMON NAME: Black-throated Gray Warbler for the markings on the adult male

OTHER NAMES: None found

palmarum: Latin *palma* = palm tree. "Of the palms" refers to the trees in which the type specimen was collected on the island of Santo Domingo (Hispaniola).

COMMON NAME: Palm Warbler

OTHER NAMES: red-poll warbler, yellow tip-up, wagtail warbler

pensylvanica: A coined Latin adjective for "Pennsylvania" + suffix *-ica* = of or pertaining to. "Of Pennsylvania" identifies the locality of the type specimen taken near Philadelphia. The Law of Priority maintains the original misspelling.

COMMON NAME: Chestnut-sided Warbler for the reddish-brown stripe on each side of the breast

OTHER NAMES: golden-crowned flycatcher, bloody-sided warbler *petechia:* Italian *petecchia* (Latin *impetigo*) = reddish-purple spot, rash, freckle. "Reddish spot" refers to the chestnut streaking on the breast and underparts of the adult male.

COMMON NAME: Yellow Warbler for the plumage color of both sexes

OTHER NAMES: golden warbler, summer warbler, yellowbird

pinus: The Latin word for "pine tree" refers to the bird's habitat of coniferous woods.

COMMON NAME: Pine Warbler

OTHER NAMES: pine-creeping warbler, pine creeper

ruticilla: Latin *rutilus* = red (inclining to yellow) + the spurious suffix -*cilla* = tail. "Red-tailed" refers to the reddish-orange on the tail, wings, and sides of the adult male.

COMMON NAME: American Redstart distinguishes this species from the Eurasian redstarts. "Redstart" is an anglicized word from the German *roth* = red + *stert* = tail.

OTHER NAMES: redstart flycatcher, yellow-tailed warbler, butterfly bird, fire-tail

striata: A form of Latin *striāre* = to groove, striate. "Striated" refers to the black streaks on the back and sides.

COMMON NAME: Blackpoll Warbler for the dark cap on top of the head (poll)

OTHER NAMES: black-poll, autumn warbler

tigrina: The Latin word for "tigerlike, marked like a tiger [*tigris*]" alludes to the conspicuous dark streaks on the breast and sides of these birds.

COMMON NAME: Cape May Warbler for the locality of the type specimen taken in Cape May County, New Jersey

OTHER NAME: spotted creeper

townsendi: A Latin form of "Townsend's." This bird is named for John K. Townsend (see *Myadestes townsendi*).

COMMON NAME: Townsend's Warbler

OTHER NAMES: None found

virens: A form of the Latin verb *virēre*, meaning "to be green," describes the bright olive-green back and crown.

COMMON NAME: Black-throated Green Warbler for the distinctive throat color and the olive-green upperparts

OTHER NAMES: green black-throated flycatcher, evergreen warbler

SIALIA: A coined noun from the Greek *sialis* = a kind of bird (perhaps with a sweet song), according to the Greek grammarian and author Athenaeus (fl. A.D. 200). Arnott suggests that the word may come from the Greek *sialon* (spittle) and *sializein* (to slather, sputter), which, according to Coues and Edward S. Gruson, imply a sibilant sound. THRUSH FAMILY.

currucoides: From Latin *curruca* = hedge sparrow (according to the Roman satirist Juvenal) + Greek suffix *-oides* = similar to, resembling. The naming of this species is attributed to Johann Matthäus Bechstein (1757–1822), a German naturalist and forester, who identified this bird from a specimen in hand. "*Curruca*-like" implies that Bechstein considered this species to possess the characteristics of one or more of the many birds classified as *Curruca*, a former genus that contained more than 400 species, including warblers, finches, and others.

COMMON NAME: Mountain Bluebird for the breeding range in the western United States and the striking turquoise-blue plumage

OTHER NAMES: Rocky Mountain bluebird, arctic bluebird

mexicana: A latinized adjective form for "of Mexico," where the type specimen was collected.

COMMON NAME: Western Bluebird for the breeding range in the United States and the mostly dark blue upperparts

OTHER NAMES: chestnut-backed bluebird, Mexican bluebird

sialis: See genus description for *Sialia.*

COMMON NAME: Eastern Bluebird for the range east of the Rocky Mountains and for the bright blue upperparts

OTHER NAMES: blue robin, blue redbreast, common bluebird

SITTA: From Greek *sittē,* meaning "nuthatch" (Aristotle). NUTHATCH FAMILY.

canadensis: Coined Latin adjective for "Canada" + suffix *-ensis* = of or from a place. "Of Canada" pertains to the region where the type specimen was collected.

COMMON NAME: Red-breasted Nuthatch for the rust-colored underparts

OTHER NAMES: red-bellied nuthatch, topsy-turvy-bird, Canada nuthatch

carolinensis: Coined Latin adjective for "Carolina" + suffix *-ensis* = of or from a place. "Of Carolina" applies to the location of the type specimen taken in South Carolina.

COMMON NAME: White-breasted Nuthatch for the pale underparts

OTHER NAMES: devil-down-head, tree mouse, topsy-turvy-bird, yank (for call)

pusilla: The Latin word for "very small" alludes to the size.

COMMON NAME: Brown-headed Nuthatch for the large, brownish cap of both the male and female

OTHER NAME: gray-headed nuthatch

pygmaea: From Greek *pygmaios* = a measure of length, about one foot; in Pliny, Ovid, and others the *Pygmaei* are a race of small people in Africa. Both the Greek and Latin words came to connote "smallness." The term "pygmy," then, is a fitting description of this smallest of the nuthatches.

COMMON NAME: Pygmy Nuthatch

OTHER NAMES: pine nuthatch, white-naped nuthatch, black-eared nuthatch

SOMATERIA: From Greek *sōma, sōmatos* (genitive) = body + *erion* = wool. "Woolly body" affirms the soft, dense down for which birds in this genus are famous. DUCK FAMILY.

mollissima: The Latin word for "softest" is an appropriate description for the superlative down of this species.

COMMON NAME: Common Eider for this most far-ranging eider and thus the most commonly seen

OTHER NAMES: northern eider, husky duck, shore duck

spectabilis: The Latin word for "worth seeing, remarkable, showy" refers to the striking colors and plumage pattern of the adult male.

COMMON NAME: King Eider. Most sources suggest that the male's large, orange frontal lobe is comparable to the crown of a king; the red, orange, blue, green, black, and white plumage of the adult male evokes the image of a royal robe of many colors.

OTHER NAMES: king drake, king duck, sea-duck

SPHYRAPICUS: From Greek *sphyra* = hammer, mallet + Latin *picus* = woodpecker. "Hammering woodpecker" characterizes the feeding behavior and nest-building technique of birds in this genus. WOODPECKER FAMILY.

nuchalis: From postclassical Latin *nucha* = neck, nape + suffix *-alis* = pertaining to. "Naped" locates the varying red and black markings on the back of the neck of both male and female.

COMMON NAME: Red-naped Sapsucker

OTHER NAMES: None found

thyroideus: From Greek *thyreos* = large oblong shield + suffix *-oides* = similar to, resembling. "Shield-shaped" describes the black patch on the breast of the female.

COMMON NAME: Williamson's Sapsucker. The common name was given to this bird by John S. Newberry (1822–1892), a physician and geologist, for his colleague Robert Stockton Williamson (1824–1882). Williamson, a graduate of West Point, was a military engineer who conducted several important surveying expeditions in the American West.

OTHER NAMES: Williamson's woodpecker, black-crowned sapsucker

varius: The Latin word for "variegated, with diverse colors, mottled" describes the black-and-white barring on the body and wings.

COMMON NAME: Yellow-bellied Sapsucker for the yellowish wash on the underparts of this species, which drills rows of small holes in trees to feed on the sap

OTHER NAMES: yellow-belly, red-throated sapsucker, sap sipper

SPINUS: This is a Latin form of the Greek word *spinos,* which was Aristotle's word for "a small, finchlike bird." FINCH FAMILY.

pinus: The Latin word for "pine tree" refers to the habitat of conifer trees whose seeds are the preferred diet of this species.

COMMON NAME: Pine Siskin for habitat; and an onomatopoetic name that, according to Coues, occurs in many languages for the sharp call note, e.g., Swedish *siska* and Danish *sidsken*.

OTHER NAMES: pine finch, northern canary bird, American siskin

psaltria: The Latin and Greek word for "a lute [*psalter*] player" alludes to the rambling, melodic song.

COMMON NAME: Lesser Goldfinch for a species that is smaller than other goldfinches in the United States

OTHER NAMES: dark-backed goldfinch, green-backed goldfinch, Arkansas goldfinch

tristis: The Latin word for "mournful, sad" refers to the long, soft, sweet song, which Linnaeus apparently perceived as mournful.

COMMON NAME: American Goldfinch, which distinguishes this species from the Eurasian Goldfinch (*Carduelis carduelis*)

OTHER NAMES: wild canary, thistle bird, yellowbird

SPIZA: This Greek word for "finch" (from *spizein* = to chirp, peep) was applied by Aristotle to several birds. SPARROW FAMILY.

americana: A latinized adjective form of "America" that denotes the range of this bird in the Western Hemisphere.

COMMON NAME: Dickcissel, which is onomatopoetic

OTHER NAMES: black-throated bunting, little meadowlark

SPIZELLA: From Greek *spiza* = finch + Latin diminutive suffix *-ella*. "Little finch" is an arbitrary description of size. SPARROW FAMILY.

arborea: The Latin word for "of trees" describes the usual habitat.

COMMON NAME: American Tree Sparrow for its range and habitat

OTHER NAMES: winter sparrow, snow chippy, winter chip-bird

breweri: A latinized form of "Brewer's." This bird is named for Thomas M. Brewer.

COMMON NAME: Brewer's Sparrow

OTHER NAME: roadrunner

pallida: The Latin word for "pale, light-colored" describes the clean, buffy underparts in nonbreeding plumage and the generally "lighter" look.

COMMON NAME: Clay-colored Sparrow for the pale brown and gray upperparts

OTHER NAMES: None found

passerina: From Latin *passer* = sparrow + diminutive suffix *-ina*. "Little sparrow" refers to its perceived diminutive size.

COMMON NAME: Chipping Sparrow for the trilled song and call note

OTHER NAMES: chippy, chip-bird, social sparrow

pusilla: The Latin word for "very little" refers to size, but this bird is no smaller than most sparrow species.

COMMON NAME: Field Sparrow for its general grassland habitat

OTHER NAMES: bush sparrow, ground-bird

STELGIDOPTERYX: From Greek *stelgis, stelgidos* (genitive) = scraper, strigil + *pteryx* = wing. "Scraper wing" refers to the "barbed" structure of the outermost primary feathers.
SWALLOW FAMILY.

serripennis: From Latin *serra* = a saw + *penna* = feather or wing. "With serrated wings" is a Latin version of the genus name.

COMMON NAME: Northern Rough-winged Swallow, which distinguishes this species from its southern (tropical) counterpart, *S. ruficollis*; rough-winged for the structure of the primaries

OTHER NAMES: rough-wing, gully martin, bridge swallow

STERCORARIUS: From Latin *stercus, stercoris* (genitive) = dung, excrement + suffix *-arius* = pertaining to. "Having to do with offal" refers to the diet of carrion and food disgorged by other birds. JAEGER FAMILY.

longicaudus: From Latin *longus* = long + *cauda* = tail. "Long tail" emphasizes the streaming central tail feathers of the adult birds.

COMMON NAME: Long-tailed Jaeger

OTHER NAMES: arctic jaeger, gull-teaser, whip-tail

parasiticus: The Latin word for "parasitic" describes this scavenger, which eats food disgorged by other birds.

COMMON NAME: Parasitic Jaeger

OTHER NAMES: arctic skua, dung hunter, man-o'-war

pomarinus: From Greek *pōma, pōmatos* (genitive) = lid, cover + *rhis, rhinos* (genitive) = nose. "Nose cover" pertains to a rim that forms at the base of the beak, covering the nostrils in breeding season.

COMMON NAME: Pomarine Jaeger

OTHER NAMES: pomarine skua, sea robber, gull-chaser

STERNA: This postclassical Latin word comes from Old English *stearn* = tern, swallow. TERN FAMILY.

forsteri: A latinized form of "Forster's." This bird was named for Johann Reinhold Forster (1729–1798), a German Lutheran pastor and naturalist who was active in America and Canada and who wrote prolifically of the flora and fauna in the Americas. Significant for ornithology are his *Catalogue of the Animals of North America* (1771) and *An Account of the Birds Sent from Hudson's Bay* (1772).

COMMON NAME: Forster's Tern

OTHER NAMES: high diver, marsh tern, sea swallow

hirundo: The Latin word for "a swallow." The name "sea swallow" for any tern is common. The forked tail and swift, graceful flight are characteristic of both birds.

COMMON NAME: Common Tern, which is abundant on both coasts and inland lakes and the most commonly seen tern in the United States

OTHER NAMES: red shank, striker, Lake Erie gull, sea swallow

paradisaea: Postclassical Latin word from Greek *paradeisos* = park, pleasure ground. This word was used in the Septuagint for the Garden of Eden and later for the concept of heaven. Could this bird be named for its out-of-this-world beauty or for its miraculous migratory path?

COMMON NAME: Arctic Tern for its far-northern breeding range, from which it launches its long annual migration to the Antarctic

OTHER NAMES: paradise tern, crimson-billed tern, long-tailed tern, short-footed tern, sea swallow

STERNULA: This postclassical Latin word comes from the Old English *stearn* = tern, swallow + diminutive suffix *-ula*. "Little tern" pertains to the petite size. TERN FAMILY.

antillarum: This Latin word for "of the Antilles" identifies the locality of the type specimen collected on Guadeloupe in the Lesser Antilles.

COMMON NAME: Least Tern, the smallest of all the American terns

OTHER NAMES: silvery tern, little striker, minute tern, sea swallow

STREPTOPELIA: From Greek *streptos* = collar, necklace + *peleia* = a kind of dove or pigeon. "Collared dove" alludes to the small black and buffy "scarf" on the nape of the adult. DOVE FAMILY.

decaocto: From the Latin prefix *deca* = ten (*decem*) + *octo* = eight. Several sources cite the Greek myth in which Decaocto (meaning "Eighteen"), a lovely handmaiden, prayed for release from her cheerless existence. The gods obligingly changed her into a dove. The call of this species is supposedly a version of her name, although perhaps not recognizable.

COMMON NAME: Eurasian Collared-Dove, introduced to the United States from its native Eurasia

OTHER NAMES: None found

STRIX: Both Greek and Latin for "owl" (from Greek *strizein* = to make a shrill, piercing sound; Latin *stridēre*). "Screecher" is an inaccurate rendition of the regular, low-pitched calls of birds in this genus. OWL FAMILY.

nebulosa: The Latin word for "misty, cloudy" is a poetic allusion to the gray plumage.

COMMON NAME: Great Gray Owl for the size of this largest owl in North America and for the plumage color

OTHER NAMES: gray ghost, spruce owl, spectral owl

varia: The Latin word for "multicolored, variegated" describes the vertical and horizontal streaking of the brown-and-white plumage.

COMMON NAME: Barred Owl for the plumage patterns

OTHER NAMES: round-headed owl, laughing owl, wood owl, hoot owl

STURNELLA: From Latin *sturnus* = starling + diminutive suffix *-ella*. "Small starling" is misleading, since the birds in this genus are larger than a starling. MEADOWLARK FAMILY.

magna: The Latin word for "large" confirms that this bird is larger than a "small starling." Some scientific names can be confusing.

COMMON NAME: Eastern Meadowlark for its range in the United States

OTHER NAMES: common lark, meadow bird, field lark

neglecta: Latin word for "neglected" (from *neglegere* = to slight, neglect). Audubon named this species, which had not been identified as separate from *S. magna* for almost a century. Thinking that this species had been overlooked by ornithologists, Audubon assigned the name *neglecta*. The Latin words *legere* (to collect) and *neglegere* (not to collect) express well the late recognition of this bird.

COMMON NAME: Western Meadowlark for its general range in the United States

OTHER NAMES: prairie lark, common meadowlark, field lark of the West

STURNUS: The Latin word for "starling." BLACKBIRD FAMILY.

vulgaris: The Latin word for "ordinary, common" is a fitting name for this ubiquitous species.

COMMON NAME: European Starling. About 100 European starlings were released in Central Park, New York City, in 1890 and 1891 by Eugene Schieffelin (1827–1906), president of the American Acclimatization Society. It was the plan of this group to introduce to the United States all the species mentioned in the works of William Shakespeare. In the case of the starling, this plan succeeded. Only one starling, however, appears in all of Shakespeare's plays and is portrayed as a remarkable mimic (*Henry IV*, Part I, 1, 3).

OTHER NAMES: blackbird, common starling, English starling, church martin

SURNIA: The derivation and meaning of this word are uncertain. The name was given to this owl genus by André Marie Constant Duméril (1774–1860), a French zoologist, in his *Zoologie Analytique* (1806). But the name may first have been used by Mathurin Jacques Brisson (1723–1806), an influential French ornithologist and taxonomist, in his six-volume *Ornithologie* (1760–1763). OWL FAMILY.

ulula: Pliny's onomatopoetic Latin word for "screech owl" (from *ululāre* = to wail, call mournfully) describes here the notes, whistles, and alarm calls of this species.

COMMON NAME: Northern Hawk Owl for its boreal range and for the face, long tail, tapered wings, posture, flight, and diurnal activity—all of which resemble those of a hawk

OTHER NAMES: hawk owl, day owl, Canadian owl

TACHYCINETA: Coined from Greek *tachys* = swift, quick, fleet + *kinētēs* = a mover (from *kinein* = to move). "Fast mover" expresses the speedy flight. SWALLOW FAMILY.

bicolor: This Latin word for "two-colored" highlights the iridescent blue-green upperparts and clean white underparts of the adult.

COMMON NAME: Tree Swallow for a bird that nests in tree cavities and frequently perches on snags over or near water

OTHER NAMES: water swallow, blue-backed swallow, white-breasted swallow

thalassina: The Latin word for "sea-green" refers to the violet-green crown and greenish back of the adult male.

COMMON NAME: Violet-green Swallow

OTHER NAMES: None found

THALASSEUS: A latinized form of the Greek *thalassios*, "belonging to the sea [*thalassa*]," is an appropriate adjective for this genus, which is truly at home over and on the water. TERN FAMILY.

maximus: The Latin word for "largest" refers to size, although this species is not the largest tern.

COMMON NAME: Royal Tern for its impressive size and crest

OTHER NAMES: redbill, big striker

sandvicensis: A latinized form of "Sandwich" (in Kent, England) + suffix *-ensis* = of or from a place. "Of Sandwich" identifies where the type specimen was collected in England.

COMMON NAME: Sandwich Tern

OTHER NAMES: Kentish tern, sea swallow

THRYOMANES: From Greek *thryon* = rush, reed + *manēs* = a kind of cup. "Reed cup" defines the shape of the small nest, which is built in cavities, seldom in reeds. WREN FAMILY.

bewickii: A latinized form of "Bewick's." This bird was named by Audubon for Thomas Bewick (1773–1828), a British engraver and illustrator of the *History of British Birds*, which appeared in two volumes: *Land Birds* (1797) and *Water Birds* (1804).

COMMON NAME: Bewick's Wren

OTHER NAMES: long-tailed wren, sooty wren

THRYOTHORUS: From Greek *thryon* = rush, reed + *thouros*, a form of the verb *thrōskein* = to leap up, spring, jump at. "Reed jumper" implies a preference for water and the quick flitting activity in undergrowth. WREN FAMILY.

ludovicianus: A postclassical Latin adjective for *Ludovicus* (Louis XIV), meaning "of Louisiana," identifies the locality of the type specimen collected near New Orleans.

COMMON NAME: Carolina Wren for that part of its range in the southeastern United States

OTHER NAMES: teakettle bird (for call), mocking wren

TOXOSTOMA: From Greek *toxon* = a bow + *stōma* = mouth. "Bowed mouth" describes the shape of the curved beak. THRASHER FAMILY.

curvirostre: From Latin *curvus* = bent, curved + *rostrum* = beak, bill. "With a curved beak" affirms the shape of the bill.

COMMON NAME: Curve-billed Thrasher

OTHER NAME: Palmer's thrasher

rufum: The Latin word for "reddish" refers to the reddish-brown color of the upperparts.

COMMON NAME: Brown Thrasher for the plumage color of this slender, long-tailed bird known for its mimicry

OTHER NAMES: thrasher, brown mocker, fox-colored thrush, ground thrush

TRINGA: From the Greek word *tryngas*, the name for "a waterside bird" in Aristotle's *Historia Animalium*. A variant reading, *pygargos*, meaning "white rump," is described as a thrush-sized bird that wags its tail. *Tringa* includes species with the features described in both variant readings. SANDPIPER FAMILY.

flavipes: From Latin *flavus* = yellow, golden + *pes* = foot. "Yellow foot" affirms the color of the feet and legs.

COMMON NAME: Lesser Yellowlegs for this bird that is smaller than *T. melanoleuca*

OTHER NAMES: common yellowlegs, little yellowlegs, summer yellowlegs, lesser yellow-shank

melanoleuca: From Greek *melas, melanos* (genitive) = black + *leukos* = white. "Black and white" alludes to the checked upperparts of the adult in breeding plumage.

COMMON NAME: Greater Yellowlegs for this species, which is larger than *T. flavipes*

OTHER NAMES: big yellowlegs, winter yellowlegs, greater yellow-shank

semipalmata: From Latin prefix *semi-* = half + *palmatus* = shaped like the palm of a hand (with fingers spread), i.e., webbed. "Half-webbed" refers to the structure of the foot and toes.

COMMON NAME: Willet, which is onomatopoetic

OTHER NAMES: white wing, bill-willie, pill-will (for call)

solitaria: The Latin word for "alone, solitary" applies to this species that is frequently seen singly or in pairs.

COMMON NAME: Solitary Sandpiper

OTHER NAMES: green sandpiper, barnyard plover, peet-weet (for call)

TROGLODYTES: From Greek *trōglodytēs,* "one who enters into holes or caves [*trōglē*]," which refers to the behavior of birds of this genus, whose nests are usually placed in a hole, cavity, crevice, or hollow. WREN FAMILY.

aedon: The Greek word for "nightingale, songstress." In Greek myth, Queen Aedon, who had mistakenly killed her son, was turned into a nightingale by Zeus to assuage her grief. The allusion here is to the pleasing song of the wren, which is likened to that of a nightingale.

COMMON NAME: House Wren for its presence near human habitation and, perhaps, for its nests in wren houses

OTHER NAMES: common wren, Jenny wren, brown wren

hiemalis: The Latin word for "pertaining to winter" applies to the northern breeding range (and the winter range in the southeastern United States). This species is frequently seen in the Upper Midwest before other wrens return from the South.

COMMON NAME: Winter Wren

OTHER NAMES: Alaska wren, short-tailed wren, wood wren

TRYNGITES: From Greek *tryngas* (see *Tringa*) + suffix *-itēs* = having the nature of. "*Tringa*-like" points out the similar characteristics of these two genera, e.g., leg color and plumage patterns. SANDPIPER FAMILY.

subruficollis: From Latin *subrufus* = somewhat reddish + postclassical *collis* = neck (*collum*). "Slightly reddish neck" is a general description of the orangish-yellow, buffy breast and underparts.

COMMON NAME: Buff-breasted Sandpiper

OTHER NAMES: grass-bird, robin snipe

TURDUS: The Latin word for "thrush." THRUSH FAMILY.

migratorius: Coined from Latin *migrator* = one who changes residence + suffix *-ius* = having the quality of. "Wandering" is an appropriate adjective for this species found throughout the United States.

COMMON NAME: American Robin, which distinguishes this American bird from the several tropical robin species in the Western Hemisphere

OTHER NAMES: robin redbreast, migratory thrush, northern robin, chirrup (for call)

TYMPANUCHUS: From Greek *tympanon* = kettle drum + *echein* = to have. "Drum bearing" alludes to the inflatable air sacs (*tympani*) on each side of the neck, which produce a long, hollow, "booming" sound. GROUSE FAMILY.

cupido: The Latin word for "love, lust, desire." According to Coues, however, the word describes the feathers erected during the mating display, which resemble the wings of Cupid, usually depicted as a little boy with wings. But the word may simply mean "amorous."

COMMON NAME: Greater Prairie-Chicken for the comparison in size to the Lesser Prairie-Chicken (*T. pallidicinctus*), for the habitat, and for the appearance

OTHER NAMES: common prairie chicken, square-tailed grouse, prairie grouse

pallidicinctus: From Latin *pallidus* = pale + *cinctus* = girdled, belted. "Palely girdled" describes the generally lighter color and barring than that of *T. cupido.*

COMMON NAME: Lesser Prairie-Chicken for the comparison in size to the Greater Prairie-Chicken (*T. cupido*), for the habitat, and for the appearance

OTHER NAMES: prairie hen, prairie grouse, pinnated grouse

phasianellus: From Greek *Phasianos* = the Phasis River bird, i.e., a pheasant + diminutive suffix *-ellus.* "Little pheasant" is an obvious description of this bird, which is thought to look like a small pheasant (see *Phasianus*).

COMMON NAME: Sharp-tailed Grouse for the spikelike tail feathers erected during the courtship display by the adult male

OTHER NAMES: spike-tail, pin-tail, brush grouse, blackfoot

TYRANNUS: The Latin word (Greek *tyrannos*) for "tyrant, despotic ruler, absolute monarch" expresses the dominating, aggressive behavior of birds in this genus. FLYCATCHER FAMILY.

forficatus: From Latin *forfex, forficis* (genitive) = scissors, shears + suffix -*atus* = having the nature of. "Scissorlike" describes the very long forked tail.

COMMON NAME: Scissor-tailed Flycatcher

OTHER NAMES: swallow-tailed flycatcher, Texan bird of paradise

savana: A latinized form of the Taíno (Caribbean) *zahana* and Spanish *zavana* for "savanna" refers to the habitat of open country, pastures, and meadows.

COMMON NAME: Fork-tailed Flycatcher for the deeply forked, streaming tail

OTHER NAME: swallow-tailed flycatcher

tyrannus: A tautonym.

COMMON NAME: Eastern Kingbird for the original range, now expanded west to the Rocky Mountains and beyond; Kingbird is an appropriate translation of *tyrannus.*

OTHER NAMES: tyrant flycatcher, field martin, bee bird

verticalis: A coined adjective from Latin *vertex, verticis* (genitive) = top or crown of head + suffix -*alis* = pertaining to. "Crowned" alludes to the infrequently seen reddish-orange patch on the top of the head.

COMMON NAME: Western Kingbird for the generally western range; Kingbird is an appropriate translation of *tyrannus.*

OTHER NAMES: Arkansas kingbird, flycatcher, bee bird

vociferans: The Latin word for "crying out, shouting aloud" (from *vociferāri* = to shout out) is an expression of the sometimes loud, harsh call.

COMMON NAME: Cassin's Kingbird, named for John Cassin

OTHER NAMES: None found

TYTO: From Greek *tytō*, an onomatopoetic name for "night owl." OWL FAMILY.

alba: This Latin word for "white" describes the overall pale color of this bird, especially the white underparts of the adult male and the white facial disks of both male and female.

COMMON NAME: Barn Owl for the nesting sites, frequently in barns

OTHER NAMES: monkey-faced owl, steeple owl, golden owl

VERMIVORA: From Latin *vermis* = worm + *vorāre* = to devour, swallow up. "Worm eater" is misleading, since the diet consists mostly of insects. WARBLER FAMILY.

chrysoptera: From Greek *chryseos* = golden, gold-colored + *pteron* = feather, wing. "Gold wing" refers to the bright gold patch on the wings.

COMMON NAME: Golden-winged Warbler

OTHER NAMES: blue golden-winged warbler, golden-winged flycatcher, golden-winged swamp warbler

cyanoptera: From Greek *kyaneos* = dark blue + *pteron* = feather, wing. "Blue wings" describes the blue-gray wings (with two light wing bars).

COMMON NAME: Blue-winged Warbler

OTHER NAMES: blue-winged yellow warbler, blue-winged swamp warbler

VIREO: The Latin word (from *virēre* = to be green) is used by Pliny for "a small (green) bird." VIREO FAMILY.

bellii: A latinized form for "Bell's." Audubon named this bird for his friend John Graham Bell (1812–1889), an American taxidermist and bird collector.

COMMON NAME: Bell's Vireo

OTHER NAMES: Bell's greenlet, least vireo

flavifrons: From Latin *flavus* = yellow + *frons* = front. "Yellow front" describes the color of the throat and breast.

COMMON NAME: Yellow-throated Vireo

OTHER NAME: yellow-throated greenlet

gilvus: The Latin word for "pale yellow" describes the "wash" on the underparts of this species.

COMMON NAME: Warbling Vireo for the long, modulated song

OTHER NAME: warbling greenlet

griseus: This postclassical Latin word for "gray" describes the color of the head and nape.

COMMON NAME: White-eyed Vireo for the striking white irises of the eyes

OTHER NAMES: white-eyed greenlet, basket bird

olivaceus: From Latin *oliva* = an olive + suffix *-aceus* = having the (color) quality of. "Olive-green" is a helpful description of the greenish upperparts.

COMMON NAME: Red-eyed Vireo for the bright red irises of the eyes

OTHER NAMES: red-eyed greenlet, little hang-nest, preacher bird

philadelphicus: A coined Latin adjective for "Philadelphia" + suffix *-icus* = of or pertaining to. "Of Philadelphia" identifies the site where the type specimen was taken in Bingham's Woods near Philadelphia, Pennsylvania.

COMMON NAME: Philadelphia Vireo

OTHER NAME: Philadelphia greenlet

plumbeus: Latin word for "made of lead, leaden" alludes to the gray color of the upperparts.

COMMON NAME: Plumbeous Vireo

OTHER NAMES: blue-headed greenlet, solitary vireo

solitarius: Latin word for "alone, solitary" is the name given by Alexander Wilson to a lone migrant that he collected as the type specimen in Bartram's Woods, near Philadelphia, in 1810.

COMMON NAME: Blue-headed Vireo for the blue-gray head

OTHER NAMES: solitary vireo, blue-headed greenlet, plumbeous vireo

XANTHOCEPHALUS: From Greek *xanthos* = yellow + *kephalē* = the head. "Yellow head" describes the color of the head and breast of the adult male. BLACKBIRD FAMILY.

xanthocephalus: A tautonym.

COMMON NAME: Yellow-headed Blackbird

OTHER NAMES: copperhead, yellowhead

XEMA: A word of unknown meaning. According to Coues, *Xema* is a nonsense word coined by William Elford Leach (1780–1836), a British zoologist and marine biologist. Leach was known for his eccentric nomenclature practices. GULL FAMILY.

sabini: A latinized form of "Sabine's." This bird is named for Sir Edward Sabine (1788–1883), a British scientist who participated as a naturalist on the 1818 Arctic expedition with James Clark Ross (see *Rhodostethia rosea*). Sabine collected the type specimen west of the Melville Peninsula and sent it to his brother, Joseph, who named the bird for Edward.

COMMON NAME: Sabine's Gull

OTHER NAMES: forked-tailed gull, hawk-tailed gull

ZENAIDA: This genus is named for Zénaïde Laetitia Julie Bonaparte (1801–1854) by her husband, Charles Lucien Jules Laurent Bonaparte (see *Chroicocephalus philadelphia*). DOVE FAMILY.

asiatica: This Latin word for "Asiatic" is a misnomer, since the type specimen was taken in the West Indies (Jamaica), not India, as Linnaeus believed.

COMMON NAME: White-winged Dove for the white patch on the upper wing in flight and the white streak on the folded wing

OTHER NAMES: white-wing, singing dove, cactus pigeon

macroura: From Greek *makros* = big, far reaching + *oura* = tail. "Long tail" applies to the long, pointed central feathers on the tapering tail.

COMMON NAME: Mourning Dove for the plaintive call

OTHER NAMES: turtle dove, wild dove, rain crow

ZONOTRICHIA: From Greek *zonē* = belt, band + *thrix*, *trichos* (genitive) = hair. "Banded hair" refers to the alternating black and white stripes on the head. SPARROW FAMILY.

albicollis: Latin *albus* = white + postclassical Latin *collis* = neck (*collum*). "White neck" refers to the definitive white throat patch on both sexes of this winsome bird.

COMMON NAME: White-throated Sparrow

OTHER NAMES: white-throat, striped-bird, Canada bird, Old Sam Peabody (for call)

leucophrys: Greek *leukos* = white + *ophrys* = eyebrow, supercilium. "White-browed" pertains to the prominent white band above the eye.

COMMON NAME: White-crowned Sparrow for the white-striped head

OTHER NAMES: white crown, striped-head, scratch sparrow, jockey-cap

querula: The Latin word for "uttering a plaintive, murmuring sound" describes this species' song of drawling, quavering notes in a minor key.

COMMON NAME: Harris's Sparrow, named for the American amateur naturalist Edward Harris (1799–1863), a friend and patron of Audubon

OTHER NAMES: black-hood, hooded sparrow, mourning sparrow

Biographies

ARISTOTLE (384–322 B.C.) was a Greek philosopher and natural scientist, a student of Plato, and teacher of Alexander the Great. He founded his own school in Athens in 335 B.C., where he established the prototype of the great libraries of antiquity and lectured on many topics. He was most at home in zoology, and it was in this field that he displayed his love of orderliness and system. A keen observer and precise logician, Aristotle also possessed an intense curiosity about all natural phenomena and wrote extensively on natural science. Many of his extant works are thought to be his lecture notes, memoranda, and the notes taken by his students; all are attributed to Aristotle. In his *Historia Animalium*, consisting of 10 books, the Aristotelian qualities are manifest, for here we find an elaborate classification of the animal world. His description of birds is found for the most part in Books 7 to 9, and the citations in our text are usually from those books. Many of the birds in *Historia Animalium* are not easily identified. This uncertainty is compounded by variant readings: for example, the word used by Aristotle for a finch-sized bird that subsists on thistles is *thraupis*. Medieval manuscripts offer *thlypis* as another spelling; one manuscript spells the word *thlaupis*. Because we do not know the species of the original *thraupis* and its variant readings, we now find *thraupis* used for the family and genus of tanagers and *thlypis* for several genera of warblers: *Geothlypis*, *Limnothlypis*, and *Oreothlypis*. What is certain, however, is that Aristotle and his work have had great influence in ornithological nomenclature.

JOHN JAMES AUDUBON (1785–1851), America's best-known ornithologist and painter of birds, was born on the island of Santo Domingo (Haiti). The son of a French sea captain, Audubon was educated in France. In 1803, he came to America to manage the family estate at Mill Grove, not far from Philadelphia. Here he spent most of his time observing birds, and it was here that he introduced bird banding to America. In 1808, Audubon, newly married to Lucy Bakewell, moved to Kentucky. While continuing to observe birds, he attempted to establish himself in several businesses, all of which failed by 1820. Working his way down the Ohio and Mississippi Rivers, Audubon supported his family by taxidermy, by portrait painting, and finally in New Orleans, by teaching drawing, music, and dancing. He soon began his sole occupation of searching for birds to paint, while Lucy supported him and their two sons by teaching in Louisiana. Audubon published his famous *Birds of America*, which appeared in parts from 1827 to 1838, and his *Ornithological Biography* in five volumes from 1831 to 1839. In his extensive travels, Audubon discovered and described 25 species and numerous subspecies of birds, to which he frequently assigned eponymous names. John James Audubon stimulated an interest in and popularized ornithology in the United States by his art and prolific writing. He died in New York.

SPENCER FULLERTON BAIRD (1823–1887) was for many years secretary of the Smithsonian Institution. As a young man, Baird began his large collection of bird specimens and soon became acquainted with leading American naturalists such as Audubon, Nuttall, Cassin, and Brewer. Quiet and unassuming, Baird was well liked, and his enthusiasm for collecting flora and fauna was inspiring. During his 28 years at the Smithsonian, the natural history collection grew from 6,000 specimens to more than 2.5 million. Baird encouraged the collection of bird specimens by scores of competent people, many of whom were in government service on expeditions and surveys or in the military. In the book *Ornithologists of the United States Army Medical Corps*, Baird is mentioned no fewer than 45 times for his work with collectors such as Elliott Coues and John Xantus. For these men on the western frontier, Baird prepared *Directions for Collecting, Preserving, and Transporting Specimens of Natural History*. Cheered on by Baird, many collectors sent hundreds of bird specimens to him in Washington. His *Birds of North America* (1860) and other writings were greatly influential in American ornithology and science in general.

THOMAS MAYO BREWER (1814–1880) was born in Boston and graduated from Harvard Medical School. He soon gave up the practice of medicine to become a naturalist. Brewer's early ornithological contributions were an inexpensive edition of Wilson's *American Ornithology* and frequent submissions to Audubon's publications. He also began his wide correspondence with ornithologists at home and abroad. Like Cassin, Brewer did his work in the library and study, except when he ventured forth to collect bird eggs. Oology was Brewer's specialty, and it was in this field that he gained prominence. His most important work, *North American Oology, Part 1* (1857), was continued in *History of American Birds* (1875), which he wrote with Spencer F. Baird and the young Robert Ridgway. He left his very large private collection of bird eggs to the Harvard Museum of Comparative Zoology. Brewer was one of the combatants in the so-called Sparrow War in which he supported the introduction of the House Sparrow (*Passer domesticus*) to America, while others, including Elliott Coues, opposed this intrusion. After a long rancorous, bitter debate, Brewer's side was, alas, victorious. Brewer was, nevertheless, admired and respected for his scholarly work, his cordiality, and principles. Two species in our text bear Brewer's name: Brewer's Blackbird (*Euphagus cyanocephalus*) and Brewer's Sparrow (*Spizella breweri*).

JOHN CASSIN (1813–1869) was a prominent American ornithologist, one of the greatest of his time. While holding down full-time positions in Philadelphia as a merchant and then printing-plant manager, Cassin spent his "leisure" time in a library room, identifying, classifying, and cataloguing birds. Over the years, he described many new species from all parts of the world, 26 of which are included in the *American Ornithologists' Union Checklist of North American Birds* (1983). Cassin was a scholarly, cordial, trusted man whose work was recognized internationally. His systematic investigation of foreign birds was the first done by an American ornithologist. Cassin published many books, articles, and reports, but he is perhaps best known for his *Birds of North America* (1860), which he wrote with Spencer F. Baird and George N. Lawrence. Known for his scholarly, literate, historical approach to ornithology, Cassin was an important contributor to the classification and nomenclature of birds. Birds in our text that are named for Cassin include Cassin's Finch (*Haemorhous cassinii*), Cassin's Sparrow (*Peucaea cassinii*), and Cassin's Kingbird (*Tyrannus vociferans*). Cassin's Auklet (*Ptychoramphus aleuticus*) is found on the Pacific Coast.

ELLIOTT COUES (1842–1899) was one of America's greatest ornithologists. While in his teens, he studied birds in Labrador and published several important articles in major scientific journals. A surgeon in the US Army, Coues was posted to the Southwest in 1864. Here, encouraged and inspired by Spencer F. Baird, he collected birds and other flora and fauna, which he sent to Baird at the Smithsonian Institution. Back in Washington, Coues wrote and illustrated his monumental *Key to American Birds* (1872), an account of every bird, living and in fossil form, north of the Mexican and southern boundary of the United States. It was the first work to give a taxonomic classification of birds according to an artificial key, and it was the book by which Coues proved himself to be one of the great contributors to American ornithology. Throughout his life, Coues published prolifically on birds as well as mammals and reptiles. In the course of his unceasing work, Coues described and named many new species of birds. *The Coues Check List of North American Birds*, 2nd edition (1882) is a milestone in ornithology, and it is this book to which most of the citations in our text refer. Coues was one of the founders of the American Ornithologists' Union and was especially concerned with bird nomenclature in that organization. He helped write the AOU *Code of Nomenclature* (1886). Coues was an intense, energetic, scholarly scientist whose pursuit of truth and accuracy was unabated. Sometimes irascible and contentious, Coues was, nevertheless, respected and admired by his colleagues. For all his contributions to so many aspects of American ornithology, Elliott Coues stands alone.

CAROLUS LINNAEUS (1707–1778) was a Swedish botanist and taxonomist. He was the son of a Lutheran pastor whose teachings early on inspired young Carl's love of flowers and a passion for their names. Linnaeus began the study of medicine at the university in Lund in 1727 but soon transferred to the university in Uppsala, where he began his long journey into botany and nomenclature. Beginning with his trip through Lapland in 1732 to investigate the flora, fauna, and minerals there, Linnaeus traveled extensively. He met prominent botanists and naturalists of his day in Holland, Germany, England, and France and wrote and published during his travels. In 1741, Linnaeus was appointed to a professorship at Uppsala. There he published the important *Fauna Suecica* in 1746. Then followed the two monumental works in which Linnaeus established consistent binomial nomenclature and introduced modern scientific classification: *Species Plantarum* (1753) and *Systema Naturae*, 10th edition (1758), considered, respectively, the starting points of modern botanical and zoological nomenclature. On his tombstone in Uppsala is engraved *Princeps Botanicorum* (Prince of Botanists).

OVID, Publius Ovidius Naso (43 B.C.–A.D. 17), was born in Sulmo, studied in Rome and then in Greece, and returned to Rome, where he soon became one of the most prolific and prominent poets of his time. Ovid is well known for his *Metamorphoses*, an epic poem in 15 books. This long work is a collection of stories, almost all of which are based on Greek myth or legend. As the title implies, every story alludes to a change of shape. The citations in our text are to those stories that depict a change from human form to that of a bird, usually by divine, magical means. Begun in about A.D. 2, the poem was completed six years later, when Ovid was banished by the emperor Augustus to Tomis (now Constanta) on the Black Sea, the oldest city in Romania. Tomis was a cold, dangerous place where Ovid felt spiritually and culturally isolated. He remained there until his death. The poetry of Ovid—especially the *Metamorphoses*—manifests his profound knowledge of classical literature, which he uses as material for his fertile imagination and creative expression.

PLINY THE ELDER, Gaius Plinius Secundus (A.D. 23–79), was a Roman biographer, historian, and natural scientist. A scholar and a man of action, Pliny held both military and civil service posts and served *summa integritate* (with highest honor); Suetonius. His *Naturalis Historia* was completed in A.D. 77, two years before Pliny, commander of the Roman fleet at Misenum, sailed across the Bay of Naples to observe more closely the eruption of Vesuvius. Overcome by the noxious fumes, he died on August 24 in A.D. 79. *Naturalis Historia*, the only one of Pliny's large body of work still extant, comprises 37 books. Books 8 to 11 are concerned mainly with animals; Book 10, primarily with birds. Citations in this text to Pliny's work are from these few books. Pliny's energy and his curiosity about natural phenomena were inexhaustible. In researching *Naturalis Historia*, he writes that he examined more than 2,000 volumes containing the histories, facts, and observations of more than 100 authors. Although he has been criticized for his scientific method, his lack of discrimination, and his absurdities—for example, the cuckoo is made by changing its shape from that of a hawk, and kites suffer from gout—he is an enlightening and enthusiastic proponent of nature study. Even the title of his work has become a scientific discipline. Pliny holds a unique place in science and Western culture.

WILLIAM SWAINSON (1789–1855) was born in London and as a young man became interested in natural history. By 1808, he had written *Instructions for Collecting and Preserving Subjects of Natural History*, and he published a similar guide for naturalists in 1822. Swainson, who had a speech impediment, was most confident in speaking English, so his travels and foreign experiences were limited. He did, however, spend some time in Brazil in 1816 and returned to England with hundreds of bird specimens. Much of Swainson's work thereafter was done in a laboratory or study, where he examined bird collections sent to him by those in the field. Swainson described and published the Mexican birds sent to him by William Bullock and his son. Together with Dr. John Richardson, Swainson described Arctic species in their *Fauna Boreali-Americana* (1832), and Swainson wrote and illustrated other books concerning ornithological information. His three-volume *Zoological Illustrations* (1820–1823) and its second edition (1829–1833) were internationally admired and respected. Swainson also published works on the classification of birds, animals, fish, amphibians, and reptiles. William Swainson's work is both prolific and important. He described and illustrated many new species from all parts of the world. Those that appear in this text are Swainson's Hawk (*Buteo swainsoni*), Swainson's Thrush (*Catharus ustulatus*), and Swainson's Warbler (*Limnothlypis swainsoni*).

ALEXANDER WILSON (1766–1813) was born in Scotland, where he trained to become a weaver. In 1794, Wilson came to America and spent several years as a teacher near Philadelphia, where he was a neighbor of William Bartram (1739–1823), the renowned colonial naturalist and illustrator. Wilson learned to draw from Bartram before setting out on his decade-long quest to gather material to include in his seminal multivolume *American Ornithology*. A strong, energetic, dedicated man, Wilson collected most of his information and specimens while walking through the eastern states. He was a keen observer, precise scientist, writer, poet, and painter. Wilson was a true pioneer in the discipline, and his work influenced many early American ornithologists, including John James Audubon. Wilson has been memorialized by other ornithologists in the nomenclature of birds. His name is used in genus, species, and common names: the genus *Wilsonia* (until very recently when it was, alas, discontinued) contained *W. canadensis* (Canada Warbler), *W. citrina* (Hooded Warbler), and *W. pusilla* (Wilson's Warbler); a species named for Wilson is *Charadrius wilsonia* (Wilson's Plover); and some of the common names of the previously listed genus and species, as well as Wilson's Storm-Petrel (*Oceanites oceanus*), include his name. Alexander Wilson could be called the "Father of American Ornithology."

Selected Bibliography

American Ornithologists' Union. 1998. *Checklist of North American birds.* 7th ed. and supplements. Washington, D.C.: American Ornithologists' Union.

Aristotle. *History of animals, books I–X.* 3 vols. Loeb Classical Library, nos. 437–439. Cambridge, Mass.: Harvard University Press.

Arnott, W. G. 2007. *Birds in the ancient world from a to z.* New York: Routledge.

Baicich, P. J., and C. J. O. Harrison. 2005. *Nests, eggs, and nestlings of North American birds.* 2nd ed. Princeton, N.J.: Princeton University Press.

Behm, H. M. 1968. *Brehms heimische vögel.* Berlin: Safari-Verlag.

Blunt, Wilfrid. 2001. *Linnaeus: The compleat naturalist.* Princeton, N.J.: Princeton University Press.

Borror, D. J. 1988. *Dictionary of word roots and combining forms.* Mountain View, Calif.: Mayfield Publishing.

Brown, L. (ed.). 1993. *The new shorter Oxford English dictionary.* 2 vols. New York: Oxford University Press.

Brown, R. W. 1956. *Composition of scientific words.* Rev. ed. Washington, D.C.: Smithsonian Books.

Campbell, B., and E. Lack (eds.). 1985. *A dictionary of birds.* Vermillion, S.Dak.: Buteo Books.

Choate, E. A., and R. A. Painter Jr. 1985. *The dictionary of American bird names.* Rev. ed. Boston: Harvard Common Press.

Coble, M. F. 1954. *Introduction to ornithological nomenclature.* Los Angeles: American Book Institute.

Coues, E. 1882. *The Coues check list of North American birds: With a dictionary of the etymology, orthography, and orthoepy of the scientific names.* 2nd ed. Boston: Estes and Lauriat.

Crossley, R. 2011. *The Crossley ID guide: Eastern birds.* Princeton, N.J.: Princeton University Press.

Curson, J., D. Quinn, and D. Beadle. 1994. *Warblers of the Americas: An identification guide.* Boston: Houghton Mifflin.

Dickinson, E. C., L. K. Overstreet, R. J. Dowsett, and D. B. Murray (eds.). 2011. *Priority! The dating of scientific names in ornithology.* Northampton, U.K.: Aves Press.

Dunn, J. L., and J. Alderfer. 2011. *National Geographic field guide to the birds of North America.* 6th ed. Washington, D.C.: National Geographic Society.

———, and K. Garrett. 1997. *A field guide to warblers of North America.* Boston: Houghton Mifflin.

Earley, C. G. 2003. *Sparrows & finches of the Great Lakes region & eastern North America.* Toronto, Ontario: Firefly Books.

Ehrlich, P. R., D. S. Dobkin, and D. Wheye. 1988. *The birders handbook: A field guide to the natural history of North American birds.* New York: Simon and Schuster.

Evans, A. H. 1903. *Turner on birds: A short and succinct history of the principal birds noticed by Pliny and Aristotle.* Cambridge: University Press. First published by Dr. William Turner, 1544.

Glare, P. G. W. (ed.). 1985. *Oxford Latin dictionary.* 1982. Reprint, Oxford: Clarendon Press.

Gotch, A. F. 1981. *Birds—their names explained.* Poole, U.K.: Blandford Press.

Grant, P. J. 1986. *Gulls: A guide to identification.* 2nd ed. Vermillion, S.Dak.: Buteo Books.

Gruson, E. S. 1972. *Words for birds.* New York: Quadrangle Books.

Harrison, P. 1987. *A field guide to the seabirds of the world.* Lexington, Mass.: Stephen Greene Press.

Hayman, P., J. Marchant, and T. Prater. 1986. *Shorebirds: An identification guide to the waders of the world.* Boston: Houghton Mifflin.

Holloway, J. E. 2003. *Dictionary of birds of the United States.* Portland, Ore.: Timber Press.

Hume, E. E. 1942. *Ornithologists of the United States Army Medical Corps.* Baltimore: Johns Hopkins Press.

Jaeger, E. C. 1978. *A source-book of biological names and terms.* 3rd ed. Springfield, Ill.: Charles C. Thomas.

Jobling, J. A. 1991. *A dictionary of scientific bird names.* New York: Oxford University Press.

Johnsgard, P. A. 1979. *A guide to North American waterfowl.* Bloomington: Indiana University Press.

Kaufman, K. 2005. *Field guide to birds of North America.* Boston: Houghton Mifflin Harcourt.

Leahy, C., 1982. *The birdwatcher's companion*. New York: Hill and Wang.

Lewis, C. T., and C. Short. 1907. *A new Latin dictionary*. New York: American Book Company.

Liddell, H. G., and R. T. Scott. 1976. *A Greek-English lexicon (abridged)*. Oxford: Clarendon Press.

———. 1985. *A Greek-English lexicon (with supplement, 1968)*. 1940. Reprint, Oxford: Clarendon Press.

Lincoln, F. C., and S. R. Peterson. 1979. *Migration of birds*. Rev. ed. US Fish and Wildlife Service Circular 16. Washington, D.C.: US Department of the Interior, US Government Printing Office.

Madge, S., and H. Burn. 1988. *Waterfowl: An identification guide to the ducks, geese and swans of the world*. Boston: Houghton Mifflin.

Mearns, B., and R. Mearns. 1992. *Audubon to Xantus: The lives of those commemorated in North American bird names*. San Diego, Calif.: Academic Press.

Nybakken, O. E. 1954. *Greek and Latin in scientific terminology*. Ames: Iowa State University Press.

Ovid. *Metamorphoses*, books I–XV. 2 vols. Loeb Classical Library, nos. 42–43. Cambridge, Mass.: Harvard University Press.

Pearson, T. G., J. Burroughs, Edward H. Forbush, William L. Finley, George Gladden, Herbert K. Job, L. Nelson Nichols, and J. Ellis Burdick (eds.). 1936. *Birds of America*. Garden City, N.Y.: Doubleday.

Peterson, R. T. 2010a. *Peterson field guide to birds of eastern and central North America*. 6th ed. New York: Houghton Mifflin Harcourt.

———. 2010b. *Peterson field guide to birds of western North America*. 4th ed. New York: Houghton Mifflin Harcourt.

———, G. Mountford, and P. A. D. Hollum. 1993. *A field guide to the birds of Britain and Europe*. 5th ed. Boston: Houghton Mifflin.

Pliny. *Natural history books*, VIII–XI. 1940. Translation by H. Rackham. Loeb Classical Library, no. 353. Cambridge, Mass.: Harvard University Press.

Pollard, J. 1977. *Birds in Greek life and myth*. London: Thames and Hudson.

Pough, R. H. 1949. *Audubon land bird guide: Birds of eastern North America from southern Texas to central Greenland*. Doubleday Nature Guide Series. Garden City, N.Y.: Doubleday.

———. 1951. *Audubon water bird guide: Water, game, and large land birds of eastern and central North America.* Doubleday Nature Guide Series. Garden City, N.Y.: Doubleday.

———. 1957. *Audubon western bird guide: Land, water, and game birds of western North America from Mexico to the Arctic Ocean.* Doubleday Nature Guide Series. Garden City, N.Y.: Doubleday.

Ridgway, R. 1881. *Nomenclature of North American birds: Chiefly contained in the United States National Museum.* Bulletin of the United States National Museum No. 21. Washington, D.C.: US Government Printing Office.

Rising, J. D. 1996. *A guide to the identification and natural history of the sparrows of the United States and Canada.* San Diego, Calif.: Academic Press.

Robbins, C. S., B. Bruun, and H. S. Zim. 2001. *Birds of North America: A guide to field identification.* Rev. ed. New York: St. Martin's Press.

Sayre, J. K. 1996. *North American bird folknames and names.* Foster City, Calif.: Bottlebrush Press.

Sibley, D. A. 2000. *The Sibley guide to birds.* New York: Alfred A. Knopf.

———, J. B. Dunning, and C. Elphick (eds.). 2001. *The Sibley guide to bird life & behavior.* New York: Alfred A. Knopf.

Stokes, D. W., and L. Q. Stokes. 2010. *The Stokes field guide to the birds of North America.* New York: Little, Brown.

Svensson, L., and P. J. Grant. 1999. *Birds of Europe.* Princeton, N.J.: Princeton University Press.

Terres, J. K. 1980. *The Audubon Society encyclopedia of North American birds.* New York: Alfred A. Knopf.

Thompson, D. W. 1895. *A glossary of Greek birds.* Oxford: Clarendon Press.

Turner, A., and C. Rose. 1989. *Swallows and martins: An identification guide and handbook.* Boston: Houghton Mifflin.

Wells, D. 2002. *100 birds and how they got their names.* Chapel Hill, N.C.: Algonquin.

Welty, J. C., and L. Baptista. 1982. *The life of birds.* 4th ed. New York: Saunders College Publishing.

Williams, T. 2005. *A dictionary of the roots and combining forms of scientific words.* Norfolk, U.K.: Squirrox Press.

Internet Web References

www.aba.org (American Birding Association)

www.aou.org (American Ornithologists' Union)

www.birds.cornell.edu (Cornell Lab of Ornithology)

www.birdwatchersdigest.com (Bird Watcher's Digest: content for bird watchers)

www.fatbirder.com (Fatbirder: bird-watching resources)

www.lab.fws.gov/featheratlas (US Fish and Wildlife Service)

www.ornithology.com (Ornithology: The Science of Birds: birding information; interactive)

www.sibleyguides.com (Sibley Guides: Identification of North American Birds and Trees)

www.usgs.gov (search "birds," click on "Patuxent Bird Identification InfoCenter") (US Geological Survey)

Index of Common Names

Index of Species Names

*A Projectile Point Guide for the
Upper Mississippi River Valley*
Robert F. Boszhardt

*Wend Your Way:
A Guide to Sites along
the Iowa Mormon Trail*
L. Matthew Chatterley

*Field Guide to Wildflowers of
Nebraska and the Great Plains*
Jon Farrar

*The Guide to Oklahoma
Wildflowers*
Patricia Folley

*The Guide to Iowa's
State Preserves*
Ruth Herzberg and
John Pearson

*Mushrooms and Other Fungi of
the Midcontinental United States:
Second Edition*
D. M. Huffman, L. H. Tiffany,
G. Knaphus, and R. A. Healy

*Wildflowers of Iowa Woodlands.
Second Edition*
Sylvan T. Runkel and
Alvin F. Bull

*Wildflowers and Other Plants
of Iowa Wetlands*
Sylvan T. Runkel and
Dean M. Roosa

*Wildflowers of the Tallgrass
Prairie: The Upper Midwest.
Second Edition*
Sylvan T. Runkel and
Dean M. Roosa

*The Scientific Nomenclature of
Birds in the Upper Midwest*
James Sandrock and
Jean C. Prior

*A Dictionary of Iowa Place-
Names*
Tom Savage

The Butterflies of Iowa
Dennis W. Schlicht,
John C. Downey, and
Jeffrey C. Nekola

*Forest and Shade Trees of Iowa,
Third Edition*
Peter J. van der Linden and
Donald R. Farrar

Prairie: A North American Guide
Suzanne Winckler